What others

“Family time spent together [illegible], bonding, nurturing time – and this book shows how to make it quality time, right in our own backyard, where there are so many rich resources for families. The book is a treasure trove of great ideas for young and old alike, and an excellent resource for parents.”

William J. Cirone, Santa Barbara County Superintendent of Schools

“Recreation is what I do for a living. As hard as I tried, I couldn’t find anything left out of Dana Fisher’s book.”

Rod Tucknott, Director, UCSB Adventure Programs

“This guide is a concierge’s dream! It is so easy to use that you can be out the door towards a new adventure in minutes. Let this book point you in the direction of fun.”

Chivaun Clark, General Manager, Santa Barbara Hotel Group

“Turn off the TV and you’ll never run out of things to do with your children – thanks to *Santa Barbara Fun*, I can’t wait to explore Lizard’s Mouth, check out the Oil Seep Tour, and rent a dog to walk with my daughter! And thanks for the money saving tips!”

Tracy Lehr, KEYT TV

“Dana Fisher offers a never-before seen perspective on our beautiful town and how the children of locals and tourists alike can explore all our sea-side haven has to offer. The book is a must read for anyone with children who wants to know more about Santa Barbara.”

Jeramy Gordon, Publisher, Santa Barbara Daily Sound

“This book is a wonderful resource not only for the countless families who visit our area each year, but also for local residents who may not be aware of many of the family-oriented activities available in our own backyard.”

Jason McCarthy, Past President, Greater Santa Barbara Lodging & Restaurant Association (GSBLRA)

“This book is fun for tourists and locals alike! A great way to take advantage of all that Santa Barbara has to offer for families!”

Rachel Ross Steidl, Founder, SantaBarbaraParent.com

"Whether you are new to Santa Barbara or have lived here all your life, you are sure to find something in this book you can't wait to try."

Ellen Stoddard, Director, Lou Grant Parent Child Workshop

"Over the last thirty years, there has been a dramatic increase in obesity and related health problems in children. This book shows parents how to get their children away from sedentary activities such as television and video games and involved in enjoyable physically-active adventures in their community."

Dr. David A. Dzewaltowski
Professor & Head of Department of Kinesiology
Kansas State University

"Play is your children's work. *Santa Barbara Fun* provides the places to play and how to get there – a must for every Santa Barbara parent."

Laura Sobell
Teacher, Santa Barbara Adult Education Parenting Classes for 30 Years

"This is an inspired little book and it will quickly become a terrific resource for any Santa Barbara family – and not just newcomers! My family has lived here eight years and I learned so much flipping through its pages. Dana's book not only highlights kid-friendly destinations; he suggests many fantastic educational attractions as well. As an elementary school leader, I know this book will be a wonderful tool for both teachers and parents."

Joel J. Weiss, Head of School, Crane Country Day School

"The development of self-esteem is intimately tied to the feeling that a child is attractive as a person to his/her parents. Nothing promotes this feeling more than a parent's saying, 'Would you like to play?'

In the book *Santa Barbara Fun*, Dana Fisher captures this special attitude and offers an endless variety of excursions that promote the development of children's self-esteem, as well as the idea that involvement in family and community activities can be fun. The catalogue of "places to go" and "what to do" is extensive and informative. It will certainly broaden my horizons for time well spent with visiting grandchildren."

Dr. Paul J. Meisel, Ph.D., Clinical Psychologist

Santa Barbara Fun

For Ages 1 to 100

By Dana E. Fisher

AAAKQ Press
Santa Barbara

Santa Barbara Fun For Ages 1 to 100
Published by
AAAKQ Press
Post Office Box 50645
Santa Barbara, CA 93150
Orders@santabarbarafun.net
www.santabarbarafun.net

Book design and typography by Jim Cook
Map design by Chris Baker
Cover design by Christopher Barber
Unattributed quotations are by Dana Fisher

Library of Congress Cataloging-in-Publication Data
Fisher, Dana E.
Santa Barbara Fun For Ages 1 to 100/Dana E. Fisher

ISBN, print ed. 978-0-9791465-0-3
First Printing 2008

DISCLAIMER

We have taken steps to ensure this book is as complete and accurate as possible. Nonetheless, it is possible that it may contain some mistakes – both typographical and content mistakes. Furthermore, this manual has facts on fun that are current as of the printing date.

The design of this manual is to provide ideas on fun activities. The manual's purpose is to entertain and educate. If assistance is required in determining if a particular activity is appropriate for your child, the services of a physician, teacher or other qualified professional consultant should be sought.

Each reader of this book must assume responsibility for his or her actions while using the public or private places described in Santa Barbara Fun. Neither the author nor publisher makes any warranty or representation concerning the safety of the activities described within this book. All activities are expressly undertaken at your own risk, and at the risk of other users.

To Cha Cha and Kai

Thank you for your enthusiasm
and spirit of adventure
every step of the way.

The Children's Parade during Fiesta invites all kids.

Table of Contents

Fifth graders enjoy the view and victory of conquering Montecito Peak.

LEGEND
1 Museum of Natural History
2 Santa Barbara Mission
3 Alice Keck Park Memorial Gardens
4 Kids' World
5 Alameda Park
6 Santa Barbara Museum of Art
7 Santa Barbara Library
8 Santa Barbara County Courthouse
9 El Presidio State Historic Park
10 Paseo Nuevo Shopping Center
11 Santa Barbara Historical Museum
12 AMTRAK
13 Land & Sea Tours/ Santa Barbara Old Town Trolley
14 Maritime Museum
15 Breakwater
16 Sand Spit Beach
17 Stearns Wharf
18 Ty Warner Sea Center
19 Skaters Point Skateboard Park
20 Chase Palm Park
0 .25
Miles
Los Positas Rd
Foothill Rd
Constance Ave
Quinto St
Junipero St
Pueblo St
State St
Anacapa St
Mission Cyn Rd
Mountain Dr
Los Olivos St
Padre St
Mission St
Pedregosa St
Islay St
Valerio St
Mission Ridge Rd
Alameda
Castillo St
Bath St
De La Vina St
Chapala St
Arrellaga St
Micheltorena St
Sola St
Victoria St
Anapamu St
Figueroa St
Carrillo St
Canon Perdido St
De La Guerra St
Santa Barbara St
Garden St
Laguna St
Olive St
Ortega St
Cota St
Haley St
Gutierrez St
Milpas St
Salsipuedes St
Yanonali St
San Andres St
Chino St
Loma Alta St
Montecito St
101
Shoreline
Cabrillo Blvd
West Beach
Stearns Wharf
Breakwater
Chavez
Calle Cesar
225

Every Solstice Parade has a theme and everyone is welcome.

How to Use This Guide

This book is for the young and the young at heart, thirsting for quick and easy fun, adventure and education in the Santa Barbara area. It's about the most vibrantly enriching activities, from learning about community service, to learning about nature, culture, history, and science; simple experiences that develop the individual, and the relationship between child and parent.

Use this "Top 250" compilation of things to do around here when you don't have time to read volumes, but when you just want world-class fun and you want it *now*. Get out the door and on your way with crystal-clear instructions.

Zero in easily on something right for you or your children, viewing pictures that quickly illustrate what you'll be in for. Zoom to the type of action that most applies to you via the double-page entries with simple ratings, ages, directions and helpful tips. We haven't included C grade or average activities so as not to waste your time. "Ages" means recommended ages. It's to assist you in what might be appropriate for you or your child. Sometimes age restrictions are set by the facility you are visiting. All "Directions" time and distances start from Garden Street at U.S. Highway 101. "Contact" information is given for each activity; all phone numbers are (805) area code, unless otherwise noted. ALWAYS CALL BEFORE leaving for a destination to verify hours haven't changed and it's still open for business.

If you're a first-time visitor to Santa Barbara, start with the Top Ten Chapter: these are the entries you will generally find in any Santa Barbara guide.

If you're a long-time resident looking for something new, turn to the Under Your Nose Chapter, or Secrets of the Santa Barbarians.

Enjoy this manual with the confidence that during research, writing, photography, editing and publishing, our team received no free services or products. Trust that all information contained herein is free from surreptitious advertising, kickbacks or loyalties due to financial arrangements.

Remember, the only trips you regret are the ones you don't take. Therefore, read, call, and go!

Many love to learn about other cultures during Old Spanish Days . . .

Foreword

Outings are so much more fun when we can savor them through the children's eyes. ***– Lawana Blackwell***

You have already taken the children to the Santa Barbara Zoo. Is there anything else to do in Santa Barbara? Oh yeah! Within the pages of this book, you will find many undiscovered jewels in our beautiful area.

When Dana approached me with his idea to develop a guidebook for families, I thought he might produce a small booklet that he could distribute to the families in our cooperative school. Instead, he approached the project with creativity and zeal. He and his two children, Channing and Kai, drove, walked, hiked, biked, sailed, flew, ate, and played their way through Santa Barbara County. Now, countless adventures later, he has created this extraordinary compilation of child-friendly places.

I love that this book emphasizes simple activities. Keep the focus on the experience and let it unfold as it will – magical moments will follow. These unexpected adventures build relationships and stand out as the memorable moments of life. So, whether you are new to Santa Barbara or have lived here all your life, you are sure to find something in this book you can't wait to try. Go do it – immerse yourselves in the experience, lose yourselves in the moment, laugh together, and have fun!

P.S. Don't forget to turn off your cell phone.

ELLEN STODDARD
Parent Education instructor
Director, Lou Grant Parent-Child Workshop

El Paseo/The Presidio is the historic heart of town.

The History of Fun in Santa Barbara

"This time, like all times, is a very good one, if we but know what to do with it."
– Ralph Waldo Emerson

Fun in the Santa Barbara area began with the first visitors about 13,000 years ago. Many liked it so much, they stayed, like a lot of us! They became known as the Chumash people, and their civilization was so advanced, that recreation was a prominent part of their culture. They enjoyed sports and games, partly due to their bountiful hunting and gathering grounds. They often boated and paddled their *tomol* wooden canoes as far as the Channel Islands. They thrilled at fishing from Avila Beach to Malibu with circular fishhooks made from abalone and mussel shells. They enthusiastically hunted large and small animals in the early days with spears, and later with bows and arrows. They hiked extensively on trails they blazed.

Sailing came to Santa Barbara in the 16th century courtesy of Spanish visitor/explorer Juan Rodriguez Cabrillo. He told his friends back home and more visitors followed. The power of a good visit!

Accommodations for travelers and locals were necessary, so in the 18th century, Father Junípero Serra established the 10th of 21 Missions throughout California, and Santa Barbara Mission has since been called "The Queen of the Missions." Each Mission was designed to be one day's travel apart.

Since then, visitors have come from all over the world, and at least 10.5 million arrive in Santa Barbara annually in search of some form of the Fountain of Youthful Fun.

You are among the most current in the History of Fun in Santa Barbara. Take a moment, like the Chumash people, for recreation. Share a lively activity with your loved one(s). It's part of your heritage. Learn how the West Was Fun. . . .

Even in the County Courthouse, you can take time out for fun!

Top Ten

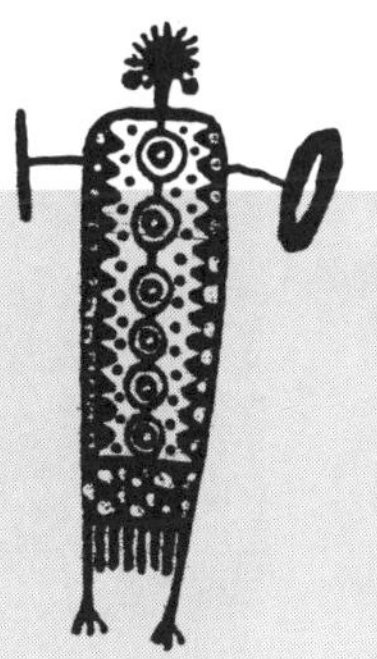

Living in the moment brings you a sense of reverence for all life's blessings. ***– Oprah Winfrey***

If it's your first visit to Santa Barbara, and you're interested in the most popular attractions, here's your plan in this chapter. If you're short on time, the absolute musts are the Santa Barbara County Courthouse, the Santa Barbara Mission, Cabrillo Boulevard bike ride/surrey ride/pedicab ride, Stearns Wharf, amphibious Land & Sea Tour or Red Trolley Tour and the harbor. Whale watching is also popular in the winter months. Santa Barbara has an incredible zoo for a city its size.

Simple pleasures include El Presidio State Historic Park and Cabrillo Boulevard Waterfront. Majestic properties like the courthouse offer outdoor wide-open spaces and castle-like interiors – custom-made for little ones' imaginations.

Highlights for children on Stearns Wharf include Ty Warner Sea Center and a ride on the darling water taxi Lil' Toot between the wharf and harbor village.

Shark bait at Kid's World.

Kids' World

Rating: A+ for active, historic, educational, one-of-a-kind
Ages: Toddler to 12
Directions: Take Garden Street inland to E. Micheltorena Street.
Contact: None
Season: Not recommended in rain

Tip: If you really want it all to yourself, go in the late afternoon/evening.

Designed by children in consultation with playground experts, then built by members of the community who volunteered their time, strength and vision to make it a reality, this is a sure hit. There is even a separate area for smaller children. If that's not enough, there are trees to climb nearby, and interesting plants. Alameda Park is one of the oldest parks in the city, and its gazebo is built in classic Spanish style, on the other side of Santa Barbara Street, where mariachi bands played in days of old, and sometimes still play today.

If you have plenty of time on your hands, you can cross Micheltorena Street and explore Alice Keck Park Memorial Gardens.

The unmistakable "Queen of the Missions."

Mission, Museum and Archeological Sites

Rating: A+ for historical, educational, cultural, beautiful, archeological
Ages: 3 to adult
Directions: Take the Mission Street exit off U.S. 101 North, turn toward the mountains, staying on Mission Street until you see signs for the Mission
Contact: 682-4149/www.sbmission.org or www.californiamissions.com
Season: Not recommended in rain, but possible!

Tip: Bring a ball, picnic lunch, blanket, or Frisbee!

Considered the "Queen of the Missions" because of its beauty and the quality of its restoration, it was founded in 1782 by Father Junípero Serra. With its world-famous twin bell towers, it boasts of a stone facade patterned after an ancient Latin temple in pre-Christian Rome. The design is traced to a book brought to California by the Franciscans – a Spanish reprint of an architecture book originally published in 27 B.C. The tenth of 21 missions built in California, it is the only one continuously occupied and used since its founding.

Visit the gift shop and museum. There is a nominal fee for the museum. Wander through the gardens behind the Mission. Check out the cemetery behind the Mission, including the grave of "Juana Maria," the Lone Woman of San Nicolas Island who was romanticized in the Newberry Medal winning book *Island of the Blue Dolphins*. She spent 18 years alone on the island 38 miles offshore. Put your hand in the fountain. Take a quiet moment for prayer inside the church.

Cross the street and chase your little one across the huge lawn, or stroll through the fragrant rose garden. Take the short hike up the hill to the old jail and ruins.

The Santa Barbara Street view of the Courthouse is imposing.

Courthouse, Sunken Gardens & "El Mirador" Tower

Rating: A+ for walk-around history, beauty, and education
Ages: Toddler to adult
Directions: Santa Barbara Street at Anapamu Street. Take 101 North, exit Carrillo Street and turn toward the mountains. Turn left on Santa Barbara Street. Go two blocks; it's a whole city block on your left at 1100 Anacapa Street.
Contact: 962-6464
Season: Docent-led tours, Mondays through Saturdays at 2 p.m. and Mondays, Tuesdays and Fridays also at 10:30 a.m. The 85' tower is open weekdays 8:30 a.m.-4:30 p.m.; Saturday, Sunday and holidays 10 a.m.-4:30 p.m. Tours are free. It's great even without the tower or tour!

Tip: Take the tour. It's one flight of stairs up to the tower. The Monday evening before Fiesta weekend (see Festivals & Events chapter) is the folk dancing dress rehearsal – before the tourists arrive! Bring your beach chairs or blanket and enjoy a picnic dinner on the spacious lawns! Also there's a free Fourth of July open-air Symphony Concert!

One of the most magnificent, and most-photographed structures in the United States. This is a must-see in Santa Barbara. The courthouse was completed about 1929 at the height of enthusiasm for the Spanish Colonial Revival style architecture. It continues to function today as the county courthouse.

Surrounded by lawns and tropical gardens, it houses hand-painted ceilings, wrought iron chandeliers, and imported tiles. Note, for visual and historic interest, the old jail building, the law library, and former supervisors' meeting room. Huge murals depict the history of the area.

Weddings take place in the large garden on a no-reservation basis; sometimes there are more than one at a time! Go to the top of the tower for the best 360-degree view of Santa Barbara.

Read the plaques on the walls for true history! Visit at night and check out the definition of good exterior lighting.

The dolphin fountain at the foot of the Wharf welcomes everyone.

Stearns Wharf

Rating: A for Fun Zone; plenty of options!
Ages: Toddlers up
Directions: State Street at Cabrillo Boulevard. 101 exit at Garden, turn toward the ocean, turn right on Cabrillo to the pier.
Contact: 682-4711 for information about the Sea Center
Season: Year-round, but generally the warmer, the better, 7 a.m. – midnight.

Tip: Allow time to eat or snack at one of the many eateries. Hold your toddler's hand; there are places with no railing on the wharf!

You could spend hours out here! This 1900-foot long wharf was originally build by a Vermont native in 1876 to accommodate ships. It's the oldest wooden working pier on the West Coast. Through the years, several fires burnt at least part of the Wharf – the most recent was a spectacular blaze in 1998. The Ty Warner Sea Center, which is located on the Wharf, is operated by the Museum of Natural History and features marine exhibits, including touch tanks that are particularly popular with children. Watch pelicans. Enjoy boat rides to see whales during winter, 969-5217. Sea lion cruises, wharf fishing, sunset cruises, parasailing, gift shops, and all kinds of food.

Local sculptor Bud Bottoms created the bronze dolphin fountain located at the foot of Stearns Wharf. There are similar dolphin fountains in Santa Barbara's sister cities Dingle, Ireland, Toba, Japan, Puerto Vallarta, Mexico and Yalta, Ukraine.

The new shark tank thrills at Ty Warner Sea Center.

Ty Warner Sea Center

Rating: A for educational, squishy hands-on, family
Ages: 2 and up
Directions: 101 exit Garden, turn toward ocean and turn right onto Cabrillo Boulevard. Turn left onto Stearns Wharf. The Sea Center is on the left.
Contact: 682-4711 or www.seacenter.org
Season: Any, as it's a great indoor activity during bad weather!

Tip: Combine it with lunch at Longboard's Grill, taking the water taxi, or just sightseeing on the wharf.

Our treasured sea center was rebuilt, updated and re-opened in the spring of 2005, thanks to the generous assistance of Ty Warner, the Beanie Baby mogul who has become well-known locally as a major property owner and philanthropist. He has purchased San Ysidro Ranch, Four Seasons Biltmore, Sandpiper Golf Course, the five-diamond Los Cabos resort Las Ventanas Al Paraiso, and Kona Village Resort on the Big Island in Hawaii.

Visitors to the sea center can experience five exhibit galleries with more than 30 marine science exhibits. It is designed to be a hands-on immersion in the work of scientists who explore, monitor and discover ways to preserve our oceans. It is twice the size of the old facility, and is part of the Santa Barbara Museum of Natural History.

Children can take seawater samples and test for salinity, temperature, pH balance, dissolved oxygen and specific gravity, and learn why these are important. They can enjoy touch tanks, a theatre, and a gift shop, as well as the view outside the facility.

Land and Sea Tours is the wildest tour in town.

Land and Sea Tours by Amphibious Vehicle

Rating: A+ for unique, entertaining, educational and amphibious
Ages: Children able to sit for 90 minutes to adult
Directions: 101 exit Garden Street, turn towards water. After .25 mile turn right into public parking lot, or cross Cabrillo Boulevard to park in lot. Walk towards the wharf, to the right on Cabrillo Boulevard. The amphibious vehicle will stop on the ocean side of the boulevard about 100′ before the wharf/State Street.
Contact: 683-7600 or www.out2seesb.com
Season: Winter tour schedule varies from summer.

Tip: Bring a sweater; it's an open-air vehicle and the last 30 minutes on the ocean can get quite chilly.

Children can't wait until this hits the water. There is only one 39'x 8' vehicle, a 2003 Hydra Terra made in New York, and it carries 49 passengers and stops pedestrians in their tracks, staring. It is DMV- and United States Coast Guard-approved. It was designed specifically for the tourist industry. You'll never forget going down the launch ramp and into the harbor. When it's in the water, you are free to get up and walk around. It's likely that you'll see sea lions from up close lying on the green buoy outside the harbor. Some say the tour guide's information is consistently the best in town.

This is also called "The Land Shark." The tour, fully narrated by a tour guide aboard the vehicle, includes fascinating notes from Santa Barbara history to houses owned by celebrities, and is delivered well; it's top-notch. It's a fun, friendly atmosphere aboard the vehicle whether it's on city streets or motoring offshore. There is little or no need for concern about seasickness, as it doesn't go far offshore; just around the green buoy marking the harbor entrance.

Old Town Trolley harks back to yesteryear.

Santa Barbara Old Town Trolley

Rating: A for information, open-air, ability to get off and ride later
Ages: 4 (if you only do half of it at a sitting) to adult
Directions: Call for directions to trolley stop nearest you
Contact: 965-0353 or www.sbtrolley.com
Season: Not recommended on rainy or cold days

Hot tips: Save money with on-line coupon, or coupon from a publication. Get off at least once, preferably about 45 minutes through, and enjoy the sights. Allow yourself time to relax and take a later trolley (ask the driver when the next and last trolley to that spot is) back to your car/hotel. Bring a sweater or coat. Your trolley pass is valid for one free boat ride aboard Lil' Toot Water Taxi.

Only San Francisco does a better red trolley! The Santa Barbara Old Town Trolley Company offers fully narrated 90-minute tours of Santa Barbara and Montecito. It looks touristy, but it's interesting even for locals. Drivers tell the history of Santa Barbara and even point out houses of world famous celebrities in the area. It's open-air so children love the wind in their hair, and adults love the information. It starts at Stearns Wharf, then stops at Cabrillo Beach Bathhouse at East Beach, Montecito Inn, Butterfly Beach/Four Seasons Biltmore, the zoo, and Fess Parker's DoubleTree Resort. It continues with the Visitor Center, Franciscan Inn, the historic Moreton Bay Fig Tree, State & De La Guerra, the Mission, Simpson House Inn (the only five-star property in the City of Santa Barbara), and the County Courthouse. The great thing about this tour is even though it's only 90 minutes long, you can make a day of it, getting off for brunch at East Beach Grill for example, and taking the next trolley behind it. You can get off and visit the zoo and get on a later trolley. You can picnic in the Mission rose garden at the halfway point, and continue after lunch. Last departure from the Mission is at 5 p.m.

A magical red engine pulls the train at the zoo.

Santa Barbara Zoological Gardens

Rating: A+ for the mini-carousel, train, playground, and a wide variety of animals.
Ages: Toddler to adult
Directions: Take 101 South; exit Milpas Street towards the ocean. After the railroad tracks, turn left on Punta Gorda to the Zoo.
Contact: 962-6310 or 962-5339
www.santabarbarazoo.org
Season: Try to avoid major holiday weekend crowds. Open daily from 10 a.m. to 5 p.m. except Thanksgiving and Christmas.

Tip: Get there early and enter at exactly 10 a.m. – go directly to see the gorillas eat breakfast! Ask at the front gate when the darling tiny carousel is open, and be sure to see it if you have toddlers. Real carousels don't get much smaller, and how often do you see a rabbit or fish on a carousel? It's an adorable antique.

The zoo first opened in 1963 with seven animals. There are now more than 500 animals living on 30 acres, including Western Lowland Gorillas, Baringo giraffes, elephants, lions (King of the Jungle gets the best ocean view!) and anteaters! Some locals go simply for the cool playground and carousel. Give the little ones some time at the playground, and let them feed the animals nearby. Don't miss the fish-eye view underground at the penguin exhibit. The cool thing about about this zoo is how close you can get to the animals. Front gate closes at 4 p.m. but you can stay until 5 p.m.

Don't hesitate to go on a rainy day: the animals are out in the rain and they love it!

Life really begins when you're at least 34" tall and big enough to ride.

South Coast Railroad Museum

Rating: A+ for HO scale trains, a real red caboose to go in, and trains you can sit on top of and ride.
Ages: 34" and taller can ride the train; any age!
Directions: Take 101 North about 10 minutes to Los Carneros Road, turn toward mountains at signal light, then go right at the Fire Station which is across the street from "Goleta Train Depot" at 300 North Los Carneros Road.
Contact: 964-3540 or www.goletadepot.org
Season: The museum is open 1 p.m.-4 p.m. Wednesdays through Sundays. The train (for people 34" and taller) runs Wednesday and Friday 2 p.m.-3:45 p.m. and Saturday and Sunday 1 p.m. – 3:45 p.m.

Tip: Patronize the store to support this non-profit organization. Ride with your children just for the fun of it! Stay until they close and watch how they store the trains indoors.

Better known as Goleta Train Depot, the museum is overshadowed by the train rides and the indoor train track with tiny trains that run over trestles designed after local ones. Check out the baggage carts. Go in the caboose and imagine what the old days were like. The closer to 34" you are, the more you will like the ride-on-top train. But it's strong enough to take adults as well. Occasionally handcar rides are available on a standard size track for larger children and adults. There is no charge for admission to the museum but there is a nominal charge for train rides. Thanks to community businesses and organizations, train rides are free some days throughout the year.

El Presidio State Historic Park is historic, educational and cultural.

El Presidio State Historic Park

Rating: B (great history but it's a brief walking tour; hands off mostly!)
Ages: Use your discretion on how interested your child will be
Directions: 101, exit Garden, inland to Canon Perdido Street, then turn left to Santa Barbara Street.
Contact: 965-0093 or http://sbthp.org/presidio.htm
Season: Daily from 10:30 a.m. to 4:30 p.m. Guided tours of the site can be arranged at De La Guerra House, or Casa de la Guerra, at the State Street end of the park, adjacent to El Paseo and across the street from De La Guerra Plaza. Open 12-4 Thursdays through Sundays.

Tip: Try to go when Casa de la Guerra is open; it could be the best part!

Founded in 1782, Santa Barbara Royal Presidio was the last in a chain of four military forts built by the Spanish along the coast of Alta California, then a wilderness frontier. Padre Junípero Serra, well known for his leadership in founding the California missions, blessed the site of the Santa Barbara Presidio four years prior to the establishment of the Mission of Santa Barbara in 1786. The Presidios played a vital role in the occupation of New Spain. They protected the missions and settlers against attack, provided a seat of government, and guarded the country against foreign invasion.

Children like the dress-up days annually in late April, during the celebration of Santa Barbara's birthday. The parties include a church service in the Presidio Chapel, reenactment of the 1782 founding of Santa Barbara, a tribute to Saint Barbara, cultural dancers, and, of course, a big birthday cake!

Built of sun-dried adobe bricks laid upon a sandstone foundation, the fort was made up of a quadrangle with two cannon bastions. Center stage was Santa Barbara's first church for its city dwellers. The Christian Chumash people worshipped at the Mission. At the State Street end of the Presidio, Casa De La Guerra was the family home for 12 children of the first commander of the Presidio. The home was also the social center of Santa Barbara for 27 years.

The Stearns Wharf cannon can conjure up historic battles.

Under Your Nose

Or, "Been there, (haven't) done that"

The foolish man seeks happiness in the distance, the wise grows it under his feet.
– James Oppenheim

Okay, so you think you know Santa Barbara from all your years living or visiting here, but have you ever:

- Made La Arcada's turtles, statues and fountains a destination?
- Sat down and listened to the drum circle on Cabrillo?
- Enjoyed quieter moments at the Santa Barbara Historical Museum?
- Taken the City Bus just for the ride?
- Walked or given a child a wagon ride out on the Breakwater, and had a picnic on the Sandspit?
- Seen and heard the Stearns Wharf cannon being fired on a special occasion?

Children of all ages, if given the opportunity to slow down and observe, love these simple things.

There isn't much that beats hand-feeding a baby racoon.

Animal Rescuer

Rating: A for "role model," or teaching your child community service
Ages: Use your discretion; 3 or 4 and up
Directions: 101 exit Garden and turn right, after about 13 blocks turn right onto Arrellaga, ½ block to 326 E. Arrellaga.
Contact: 966-0568, but no appointment required
Season: 10-5 seven days a week.

Tip: Since this is a non-profit organization, please donate your time and/or your money to help. She'll put you and your little one to work, maybe bottle-feeding a baby raccoon! And you'll both feel good about serving! Under 18 must be accompanied by parent.

Estelle Busch is one of the most fascinating people in the city. She has rescued injured birds and animals since she was a child. She literally does not have the time to write grants for money because she is so devout about her passion – being a helper. It's astounding what she has done in the past, what she has "in hand" at her facility, and what she plans on releasing back to the wild as a rehabilitated animal. She even accepts animals from strangers who know of her big heart. In fact, she accepts animals when she doesn't even know what they are. She somehow finds room for them in her small back yard. You might see owls, baby raccoons or a hawk. Sometimes Busch doesn't even know how to help. So then, she researches it until she can help. The "Hero of Santa Barbara" award goes to Estelle Busch.

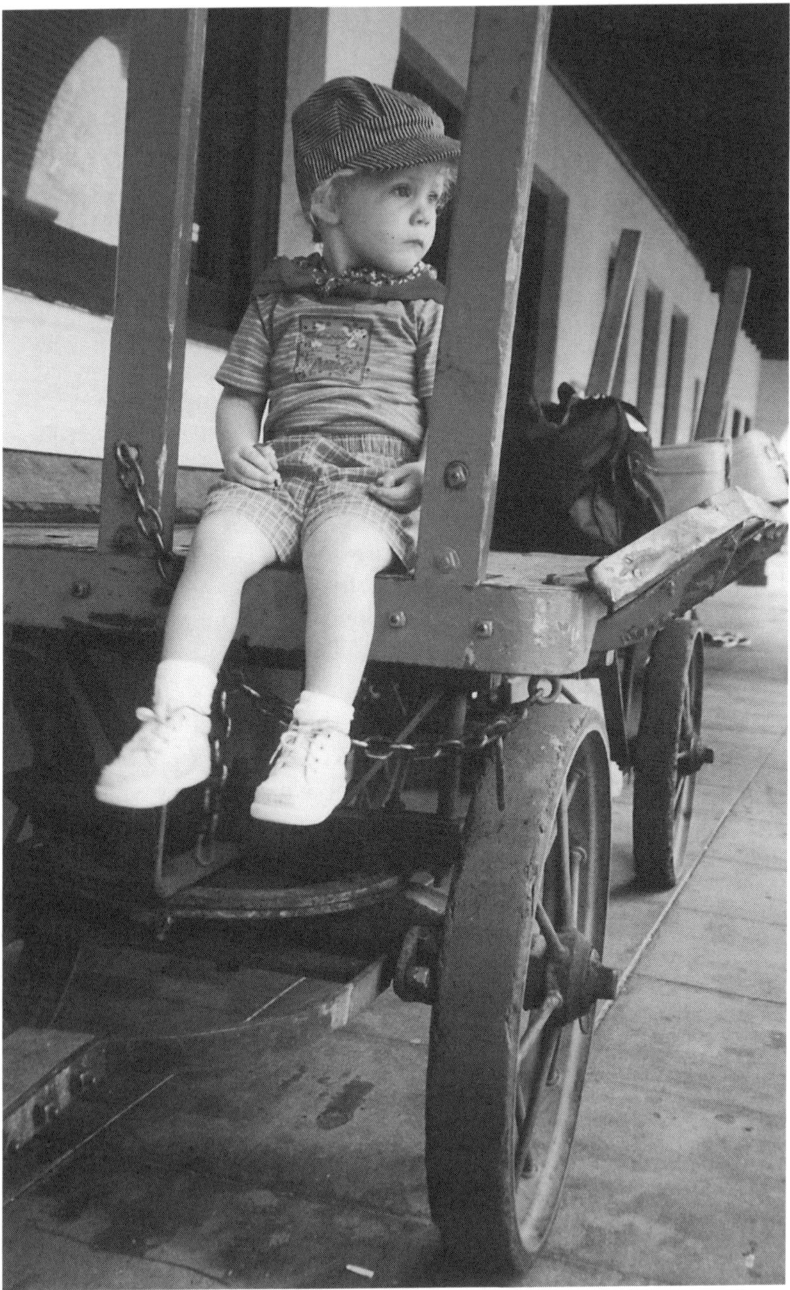

A future engineer rests on an antique luggage cart at Amtrak.

Amtrak Means Fun!

Rating: A+ for teachable moments and excitement
Ages: Toddler to adult
Directions: 101 exit Garden, turn toward the beach, then right onto Yanonali until you see the train station.
Contact: (800) USA-RAIL or www.amtrak.com
Season: Any

Tip: Get there early enough to see the train arrive. Bring a picnic lunch! During summer you can take the train to Ventura County Fair Train Station, and not have to park a car while you visit the fair. The fair usually lasts about two weeks in August, often during the same time as Santa Barbara Fiesta.

Find out when the trains go to Carpinteria, Ventura, or Goleta and enjoy a couple of hours at the beach (heading south). Then take the 20-50 minute ride back. It's a 50-minute trip to Ventura – Seaside Park/Surfers Point. On Saturday mornings, you have about an hour in Ventura before the return trip north. It's a great way to avoid driving and parking during the Ventura County Fair in August. The Ventura Amtrak station is at the fairgrounds.

Occasionally, kids can shoot the Harbor Patrol water cannon!

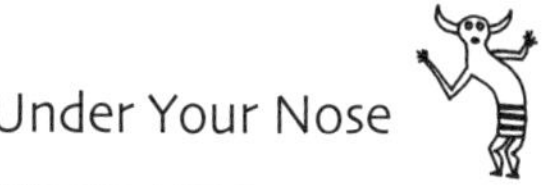

Breakwater

Rating: A for best walk in town
Ages: Bring a backpack or sling for tiny ones!
Directions: 101 north 0.5 mile, exit Bath street (Castillo). Turn left at the signal, then left again at the next signal, onto Castillo Street. Go 0.4 mile to the T intersection of Castillo and Cabrillo/Shoreline, and turn right onto Shoreline Drive. Take your first left into Santa Barbara Harbor parking lot. Walk toward the ocean on the sidewalk that skirts the harbor, toward the flags.
Contact: Sunshine and fresh air
Season: Any dry day, but the warmer, the better

Tip: If you see waves splash over the breakwater, turn back. This is rare.

After passing the Maritime Museum and restaurants, turn left onto the big commercial fishing pier and see if they're unloading any urchin boats, crab boats, or lobster boats! Local fishermen are super-friendly if you ask questions. Continue out the breakwater noting the sculpture of the boy riding the seahorse, greeting incoming mariners. It was donated by the City of Puerto Vallarta, Mexico, a sister city of Santa Barbara. Occasionally you'll see kite-boarders, sea lions, and dolphins offshore, and surfers at Sandspit Beach. An incredible walk; little ones can't go astray if your only rule is to stay on the sidewalk. You can also tow your little ones in a wagon to the end of the breakwater, where you can lock it up so that you can play at Sandspit Beach. Just follow the narrow path on the rocks out to the sand.

Hang out near the Harbor Patrol boat adjacent to the commercial fishing pier and you may be invited to shoot the boat's water cannon.

Atop a car in the airport visitor lot, you can see over the fence.

Airport Vista

Rating: A for anytime, airstrip-close, aircraft views
Ages: All
Directions: 101 North, exit Fairview Ave. Go straight through the signal light at the foot of the offramp, up over the freeway towards the ocean. In about one mile, the road bends 90 degrees to the right, putting you parallel with the airstrip. Take your first right turn, into the Airport Vista Parking Lot. It's small, but never full.
Season: Daily and nightly

Tip: Bring a pizza/picnic/ snack and do a tailgater.

There's something magical about jets or any airplanes taking off and landing. The lights are fascinating at night. The airport vehicles drive by between flights. The loud sound and the magnitude of the aircraft are spellbinding. Often little ones are begging you to stay . . .

Life imitates art at La Arcada.

Shopping El Paseo/La Arcada/Paseo Nuevo

Tip: This is a highlight for those who like downtown outings and history. Take the Downtown Shuttle from the foot of the wharf for 25¢.

Rating: A for "The Heart of Downtown," history, education
Ages: All ages
Directions: From 101 exit at Garden Street, turn toward the mountains, and turn left at Canon Perdido Street to State Street. La Arcada at 1114 State Street, El Paseo is off the 800 block of State Street at 15 E. De La Guerra St. and Paseo Nuevo is at 700-900 block of State Street
Contact: In La Arcada, Stateside Restaurant Bar & Lounge, 564-1080, if you'd like to make reservations to eat while your little ones check out the turtles in the pond, and Barcliff & Bair has nice al fresco dining, 965-5742. At historic El Paseo, it's the classic El Paseo Restaurant for Mexican food, 962-6050. At Paseo Nuevo, it's California Pizza Kitchen (see Chow Fun, Chapter 8) all the way, 962-4648.
Season: The warmer, the better!

El Paseo is the first mixed-use building project in California (1920's) and was the first kid (and fountain) on the block here. It's adjacent to Casa De La Guerra (Thursdays through Sundays Noon-4 p.m.) El Presidio Comandante José de la Guerra began building this in 1819 and the city sprung up around it. This is essential, wonderful Santa Barbara history. Next came La Arcada, one of the premier historical office/retail buildings in Santa Barbara, home to hands-on sculptures to play with and a turtle pond. It's adjacent to the Museum of Art and Santa Barbara Public Library fountain. The barbershop is first-rate, at 966-4451. The new kid on the block is Paseo Nuevo, the quadruple-fountain shopping center, which offers street performers, escalators, elevators, and numerous shops and eateries.

With UCSB students helping, youngsters learn a lot.

Touch Tanks (UCSB Marine Science Institute)

Rating: A for educational and free
Ages: 3 or 4 and up, use your discretion
Directions: 101 North seven miles, exit 217 to UCSB, and at the entrance go left onto Lagoon Road, then take your first left into Parking Lot #6. Buy a parking ticket from the machine.
Contact: 893-3765, 893-8765 or www.msi.ucsb.edu/, outreach@msi.ucsb.edu
Season: At the end of each academic quarter

Tip: If it's just you and/or your family, it's open 11 a.m.-2 p.m. Saturdays year-round, generally. Just to confirm it will be open when you plan to visit, it's best to call and ask on Friday, the day before you go, 893-8765.

The Marine Science Institute (MSI) offers one-hour tours to local community members. Participants include families, school groups, after-school programs, senior citizens, and developmentally and/or physically disabled adults. Marine Science students guide participants through a series of displays, including local marine animals and plants in lifelike habitats, a shark hatchery tank, and a tank containing fish, crabs, lobsters, sharks, and eels. Two touch tanks offer visitors hands-on experience with a variety of marine organisms including seastars, urchins, anemones, corals, and sea cucumbers. A marine mammal display allows visitors to see and touch bones and pelts. This place is a real treasure!

There are more than 100 different species of marine plants and animals housed at this Research Experience and Education Facility, better known as the REEF, UCSB's interactive aquarium facility.

Your view lying on your back during the drum circle.

Drum Circle

Rating: A for musical, inclusive, diverse, free and foot-tapping
Ages: 2 and up!
Directions: Cabrillo Boulevard/Chase Palm Park just south of the carousel, the drum circle gathers on the grass, under the palm trees.
Contact: If you want to buy a drum, contact 967-2541, www.fullcircledrums.com If you and/or your child (10 years old and up) want lessons contact Cameron Tummel 455-2599, www.rhythmsofthec.com or Arts Alive! at 1 N. Calle Cesar Chavez, www.artsalivesb.com, 963-2278. If you want drums delivered anywhere, and a leader in good fun drumming, contact him for a special group event.
Season: Saturdays at 4 p.m.

Tip: Bring your own drum and let your little one have the option of joining in! Dance with your little ones if they want to.

An eclectic group of businesspeople, students, homeless, teachers, musicians, and families get together to enjoy hours of drumming and dancing. There's something irresistible about drumming. It's primitive. It's international. It's compelling. It's fun. It's contagious. It's local. And it's by the beach under the palm trees! It's the rhythm of Santa Barbara at its best.

Steve Campbell and Lindsay Rust at Dancing Drum can bring 40 drums from Africa and the Caribbean for games, team building, or just a drumming party for your group. Mask making classes too. For more information, contact 729-0243, info@dancingdrum.com or www.dancingdrum.com or 810 E. Gutierrez St., the Dancing Drum Rhythm & Art Center.

Cameron Tummel is a rhythmic circle facilitator with RhythmsoftheC. In business since 1991, he provides drums, workshops, drum circles, and educational and corporate events. For more information, contact Cameron Tummel at 455-2599 or www.rhythmsofthec.com.

The huge whale skeleton is at the museum entrance.

Secrets of the Museum of Natural History

Rating: A for education, family-orientation, and variety
Ages: Toddler to adult
Directions: 101 North, exit Mission. Turn towards mountains. Follow signs to the mission, then two blocks past the mission are signs to turn left. 2559 Puesta Del Sol Road
Contact: 682-4711 or www.sbnature.org
Season: Daily 10-5

Tip: Don't be limited to just the museum building. Explore the trails and creek behind the museum. Bring a picnic lunch! When it's cool on the coast, it's warm here with no wind. Free admission on the third Sunday of the month. Saturdays at 11 a.m. is "The Magic Sky" for children 4-7.

Exhibits feature mammals, birds, fish, reptiles, plant life and geology of the Pacific Coast and Channel Islands. Dioramas of prehistoric Native American life. The bird nest and egg room is fascinating. Call the 24-hour Astronomy Hotline, ext. 405, for Public Sky Show information at Gladwin Planetarium. Treat your little one to something from the great gift shop . . . all proceeds benefit this historic non-profit.

It also offers weekday classes for children 2 years old and up.

If you're adventurous and nimble, you can go to the creek behind the museum and walk upstream all the way to Rocky Nook Park and return via the streets. Look for the ceramic alligators on the right bank after you pass beneath the bridge!

Youth golf clinics are the bargain of the year.

Golf Clinic for Youth

Rating: A
Ages: 7-17
Contact: 964-1414 for Twin Lakes Golf Course, 687-7087 for Santa Barbara Golf Club, www.sbgolf.com
Directions to Twin Lakes: Take 101 North about 9 miles and exit Fairview, go straight through the signal and up over the freeway towards the ocean. As you come down off the overpass be prepared for a small veer to the right before you get to the bottom of the hill, and that takes you into Twin Lakes Golf Course parking lot.
Directions to Santa Barbara Golf Club: 101 North, exit Las Positas, turn right and go about one mile. Left on McCaw to 3500 McCaw. Contact: 687-7087.
Season: Call for programs

Tip: Call regarding youth golf clinics.

What could be easier than using a flat object and hitting a ball that is motionless on the ground? What could be more fun? That's up to you and/or your child to decide! These youth programs are extremely affordable and provide an opportunity to get started in a life-long sport or just try something new for a couple of hours.

Santa Barbara Golf Club, also called Municipal Golf Course, first opened in 1958 where there was a hospital during World War II. There is a plaque commemorating that at the corner of Las Positas and McCaw. It offers golf programs for children from 7 to 17 years old. It has 18 holes. It features a PGA pro in its youth instruction program.

Twin Lakes Golf Course has nine holes – perfect for beginners – as well as an extensive golf instruction program for youth 6 and up, featuring PGA professionals as teachers. It's an incredible value.

Riders get to ring the Lil' Toot's brass bell!

Water Taxi: Lil' Toot

Rating: A for useful, centrally located, easy boating
Ages: 3 and up
Directions: On the wharf, go out to the ticket booth/dock on the left side – across from the Shellfish Company. At the harbor/breakwater, go to directly in front of the Maritime Museum.
Contact: 896-6900 or www.sbwatertaxi.com
Season: Noon to 4:30 p.m. in winter (except Wednesdays), 10 a.m. to dusk in summer (daily). Pickup times are posted at both stops.

Tip: Ask if your little one can ring the bell! All-day passes are available for adults, and children under 12 are free.

There's something special about a tugboat. And this one isn't just any old beaten up tugboat. It's beautiful. Besides transportation, it provides a fun adventure and a quick feel for the ocean and offshore views. You might see sea lions! It's a convenient link to the harbor village and the refreshing walk on the breakwater, without spending time and effort to get there. If you're a little one and you're really lucky, the captain might ask you if you want to steer the vessel!

A Crosby tugboat in bright yellow, charming to young and old. It's also a great way of seeing the waterfront from the wharf to the harbor without walking, and you might even see some sea lions on the green buoy! Captain Fred Hershman and his wife Kathy started the service in October of 2003.

Farmers' Market: the variety is fun and educational!

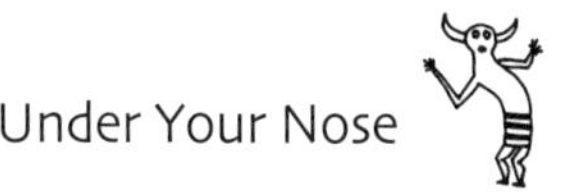

Farmers' Markets

Rating: B+ for flowers, open-air, healthy, fresh
Ages: toddler and up
Contact: 962-5354 or www.sbfarmersmarket.org
Season: All year round

Tip: Bring a sturdy bag or a wagon! The downtown market has live music.

Sundays in Goleta: 10 a.m.-2 p.m. year-round

Camino Real Marketplace: 101 North, exit Storke, turn left, then right after Hollister Ave. into the market.

Tuesdays in Downtown Santa Barbara: 4 p.m.-7:30 p.m. in Summer; 3 p.m.-6:30 p.m. in Winter; 500-600 block of State Street.

Wednesdays in Uptown: 2 p.m.-6 p.m. in Summer; 1 p.m.-5 p.m. in Winter; 101 North, exit La Cumbre Road, turn left, then right onto La Cumbre Road to the shopping center on your right.

Wednesdays in Solvang: 2:30 p.m.-6:30 p.m. in Summer; 2:30 p.m.-6 p.m. in Winter; Copenhagen Drive & 1st Street.

Thursdays in Carpinteria: 4 p.m-7 p.m. in Summer; 3 p.m.-6 p.m. in Winter. 101 South 9 miles, exit Linden, turn right – 800 block of Linden Avenue.

Thursdays in Goleta: 3 p.m.-6 p.m. year-round. 101 North, exit Patterson, turn right, then left onto Calle Real, and the market is in Calle Real Shopping Center at 5700 Calle Real.

Fridays in Montecito: 8 a.m.-11:15 a.m. year-round. 101 South two miles, exit Coast Village Road; turn left at the stop sign and curve on to Coast Village to 1100-1200 block.

Saturdays in Santa Barbara: 8:30 a.m.-12:30 p.m. year-round. Take Garden St. towards the mountains to Cota Street; turn left – one block to Santa Barbara Street. Corner of Santa Barbara and Cota Streets.

Santa Barbara Historical Museum provides educational, quiet times.

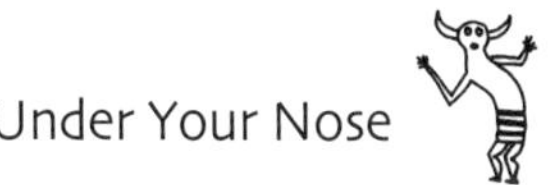

Santa Barbara Historical Museum & Gledhill Library

Rating: B for photos, educational, historical
Ages: 8 and up; use your discretion
Directions: 101, exit Garden Street; turn toward mountains; turn left at De la Guerra to 136 E. De La Guerra
Contact: 966-1601
Season: Museum: Tuesday through Saturday 10-5; Sunday 12-5.
Library: Tuesday through Friday 10-4. First Saturday of the month 10-1. Great for a rainy day too.

Tip: Call ahead to verify the hours. Not for overly active kids.

This place provides children a good one-hour fascinating destination in a classic area of town. If you like reading/history/quiet sharing/Santa Barbara, this place is under the radar but worth investigating. Group tours available if arranged in advance.

You may even want to try 20 to 40 minutes here with a child younger than 8, but take them after you've had a romp at Kids' World, for example, so they'll be ready to sit quietly awhile. There are Chumash, Chinese, Spanish, Mexican and European artifacts and various changing exhibits. There are textiles and furnishings from the 1400s. Ask for the oldest of the 45,000 pictures of Santa Barbara and things that interest children. The Gledhill Library features newspapers as old as the hard copy of the 1850 *Gazette*. A fountain outdoors graces the tree-shaded courtyard of the 1817 Casa Covarrubias adobe. It's a perfect space for a Santa Barbara-style picnic.

Public swimming pools are a great value.

Swimming and Wading Pools

WADING POOLS . . .

Swim diapers are mandatory as accidents mean the pool has to be immediately shut down. Wading pools are for children up to 7 years old.

OAK PARK, Oak Park Lane, 897-2680. May-September.

WEST BEACH, Cabrillo Blvd. at Castillo St., 897-2680. June-August afternoons.

SWIMMING POOLS . . .

CABRILLO BATH HOUSE at Cabrillo Boulevard and Castillo Streets, 897-2680 or 966-6110. During summers free swim time is available 1:45 pm-3:45 pm weekdays, and 1:15-5 pm Saturdays and Sundays. Lockers are available.

CARPINTERIA SWIMMING POOL, 5305 Carpinteria Avenue, 566-2417. Probably the cleanest and most uncrowded of all the pools. Winter hours: 6 a.m.-7 p.m. on weekdays, 12-4 Saturdays. Summer hours: 6 a.m.-8 p.m. and weekends noon-6 p.m.

UNIVERSITY OF CALIFORNIA at SANTA BARBARA pool information/schedule: 893-7616 or 893-7619, front desk or http://www.par.ucsb.edu/aquatics/rcpool.html

Seven days a week, the last day of UCSB school year through first day of classses at UCSB, there are free-swim hours and families are welcome. You can pay by the day or get a summer pass. The shallow area for young swimmers or non-swimmers is 2.5 feet deep. From the first day of UCSB classes through last day of UCSB classes in the spring, children are welcome on weekends only.

WESTMONT COLLEGE Pool, La Paz Road off Cold Springs, 565-6010, is a lap and play pool with a new diving board. You can buy a May-August pass to use the facilities rather than paying the daily rate.

ORTEGA PARK, 600 E. Ortega St., 966-6110, 3'-4.5' deep, for children younger than 13 and open only during summer.

The flat Cabrillo Boulevard bike path makes learning to skate easy.

Skating

Tip: Wear wrist, elbow, and knee pads as well as a helmet!

Rating: A if you like it/are good at it!
Ages: Use your discretion
Directions: Find the bike path anywhere from Andree Clark Bird Refuge at the Cabrillo Boulevard exit off 101, to Shoreline Park more than three miles northwest along the waterfront
Contact: If you need to rent – Wheel Fun Rentals, 101 State Street and 23 E. Cabrillo Blvd., 966-2282 or Fess Parker's DoubleTree Resort, 633 E. Cabrillo Blvd., 564-4333
Season: Dry days!

In-line skates are great, and roller skates are fun, too! Fresh air, excellent views and good exercise. If you and your children like to skate together, you'll have years of enjoyment. The rental shops also have surreys and various bikes. Look for the big bike across from the dolphin fountain at the foot of Stearns Wharf – that is Wheel Fun Rentals.

Be sure to cross busy Cabrillo Boulevard carefully.

Riding free with the wind in your hair.

Downtown & Waterfront Electric Shuttle
("The Blue Trolley")

Rating: A for an inexpensive, handy, open-air ride!
Ages: All
Directions: It travels along State Street, and the blue signs of trolley stops are every block from the foot of Stearns Wharf, up to Sola Street (1400-block). It also travels on Cabrillo Boulevard from the harbor village to the zoo.
Contact: 683-3702 or www.sbmtd.gov
Season: Year-round but it's best when the weather's warm since the glass in the windows is removed, which is most days considering Santa Barbara's weather.

Tip: Downtown Shuttle runs 10 a.m.-6 p.m. every 10 minutes. From 8:15 a.m.-10 a.m., it runs every 30 minutes. From Memorial Day through Labor Day, on Friday and Saturday evenings, it also runs every 15 minutes until 10 p.m. The price is nominal, but bring quarters! Children under 45" tall ride free. The Waterfront Shuttle runs from the zoo to the harbor village along Cabrillo Boulevard daily 10 a.m.-6 p.m. every 30 minutes, year-round.

This is the best value in town! Get off at Paseo Nuevo and let the little ones run around the mall. Bring a picnic lunch and a sweater; you never know where you will want to jump off! If your hotel is on these routes, this could be all you need to get around. The mission is about nine city blocks from the last stop. However, you walk through two city parks en route. For this adventure, walk east on Sola and diagonally across historic Alameda Park. You may be attracted to Kids' World (see separate entry in Top Ten, Chapter 1) across the street in the eastern block of Alameda Park. Walk diagonally across Alice Keck Park Memorial Gardens, then up Garden Street to Mission Street and turn right. Turn left on Laguna to the mission. The open-air trolley is a hit with locals and tourists alike.

City Bus #22 visits the most fun sites; but all buses are fun.

City Bus

Rating: B for any time or weather, educational, diverse, and hey, it's a ride!
Ages: 2-6
Directions: 101 exit Carrillo. At signal, turn towards mountains. Turn left just past the Fire Station onto Chapala. Turn right on Figueroa and right again into the city parking lot. Adjacent is the City Bus station. Or, call for the nearest bus stop near your house.
Contact: 683-3702 Monday through Friday 6 am-7 pm, Saturday 8-6 and Sunday 9-6. www.sbmtd.gov
Season: Great for a rainy day; take a long loop ride!

Tip: Just take the next bus if it's the right length ride for your child, round trip. Or, ask at the information counter, and find a destination 15 or 20 minutes away like the beach, Shipwreck Park, or Kids' World, bus there, get off and enjoy it, then return by bus. The adventurous might want to take a night bus ride!

Let's face it, we see buses daily and hardly think of getting in one, but children are fascinated by a city bus ride. Remember to bring lots of change. Children 45" tall or less ride for free. Transfers are free too. Some buses go until 9 or 10 p.m. so you can do this after work or after dinner. The great thing about it is, wherever you get off, the bus will return to a stop across the street; all you need to do is ask the bus driver when the returning bus will arrive to take you back to the downtown station.

Bus line 22 takes riders to the Courthouse, Museum of Art, Santa Barbara Mission, Museum of Natural History, and on weekends to the Botanic Garden.

This is having fun even before you even get to where you're going!

Cuyler Harbor, San Miguel Island. Don't tell!

Secrets of the Santa Barbarians

The secret of all those who make discoveries is that they regard nothing as impossible. ***– Justus Leibig***

It's the locals who consistently know when to be where in any given city. It's no different in this town. The #1 secret "where" is Lotusland, and the #1 secret "when" is the members' annual family day. Or is #1 Monday night of Noches De Ronda, the Fiesta dress rehearsal in the Courthouse sunken garden? Some say it's entering the zoo at 8 a.m. for members-only "Breakfast at the Zoo" in Spring or Fall. Others say #1 is the Thursday evening free summer concerts at Chase Palm Park.

Still others insist that on a gorgeous day, the lookout at Toro Canyon Park is the call. Every local has his or her own favorite spot. Every time they return they're more and more sure they've made the right call.

What's yours?

Be silly and dress up for free studio Polaroid portraits at Lotusland Family Day.

Lotusland

Rating: A+ for educational, outdoors, beautiful, nonprofit
Ages: toddler up
Directions: Do not go to Lotusland without a reservation. Lotusland is a public garden, which operates in a private, residential neighborhood. For reservations, call the Visitor Services office at 969-9990, between 9 a.m. and noon, Monday through Friday. When you call for reservations, they will provide you with directions.
Contact: 969-9990 or www.lotusland.org or info@lotusland.org
Season: Open for public tours from mid-February through mid-November. Children over 10 may go on regular tours. Those under 10 may go on tours on Thursdays and the second Saturdays of the month. Children get to roam free one day a year – on members' family day in April.

Tip: Even if you don't like gardens, you will love this place. The family day could be the best item in the book. It's the author's favorite event by far. It's a rare treat and worth the cost of membership.

Madame Ganna Walska is the stage name for the internationally reknowned actress and operatic singer who bought a 37-acre estate and botanic garden, and fine-tuned it to perfection over the next 43 years. Madame Walska had a passion for rare plants and was willing to pay any price for the most unusual plants. The main residence was designed by Reginald Johnson and remodeled by George Washington Smith, who also designed some of the buildings, the perimeter wall, the swimming pool which is now the lotus pond, and the adjacent bath house. You won't believe this place.

For members: One day a year, children of all ages are allowed in to attend a garden party with their families. Amazing arts and crafts for children, a storyteller in the outdoor stone-and-grass amphitheatre, a magician, live music and ice cream celebrating Lotusland's anniversary, a professional photographer with dress-up props, and much more have been featured. Minimum membership fee is $50, but the garden party is free to members.

Once upon a time, a little boy stumbled upon a pirate's cave . . .

Storytelling

Rating: A for "what's a society without storytelling?"
Ages: 3-5
Directions: Call
Contact: www.sbplibrary.org
Season: Year around, but call to verify times.

Tip: For serious storytelling for all ages, check out the Ojai Storytelling Festival 646-8907 or www.ptgo.org. It's in April.

Free weekly storytelling is available at several locations around town. In addition, all branches of the library offer incredible free summer programs, including puppeteers, magicians, jugglers, storytellers. Call or visit the web site for schedules.

Santa Barbara Public Library Weekly Storytelling Hours
Storytelling designed for children ages 3-5:

Carpinteria Branch Library, Thursdays, 10:30 a.m.
5141 Carpinteria Avenue, 684-4314

Central Branch Library, Tuesdays and Thursdays, 10:30 a.m.
40 East Anapamu Street, 962-7653

Eastside Branch Library, Wednesdays, 10:30 a.m.
1102 Montecito Street, 963-3727

Montecito Branch Library, Thursdays, 10:30 a.m.
1463 East Valley Road, 969-5063

The Red Tile Tour takes you to historic Santa Barbara.

Red Tile Tour

Rating: A- for history, education, and the essence of Santa Barbara

Ages: Your attitude and creativity make or break this. You'll think it's a joke until you WALK it!

Directions: Exit 101 at Garden, go inland on Garden to Ortega. Turn left on Ortega, go one block and park.

Contact: www.santabarbaracarfree.org for a map, which is helpful.

Season: This can be done day or night, any season. It's better during daytime when you can see the architecture, and best about midday when Casa De La Guerra Adobe and El Presidio are open.

Tip: Don't blow this off until you've tried it! It can take 30 minutes walking fast, or several hours. It's a self-guided tour.

This single tour, which is free, includes many entries in this book, such as Historical Museum, Casa De La Guerra, El Paseo, Paseo Nuevo, La Arcada, Museum of Art, Santa Barbara Public Library, Courthouse, and El Presidio State Historic Park along the way, plus other old buildings. Start on the Historical Museum side of Santa Barbara Street, then stay near the museum as you turn left onto De La Guerra Street. After you cross Anacapa Street, cross De La Guerra to see the Orena Adobe. Walk farther toward State Street and on your left you'll see De La Guerra Plaza, City Hall, and Santa Barbara News Press. On your right will be Casa De La Guerra (see El Paseo entry). Once you arrive at State Street, Paseo Nuevo is across the street. Turn right onto State Street and stay on the right side of the street. Immediately on your right will be El Paseo shops, offices, fountain and landmark classic restaurant. Back on State Street, you may prefer to pay $0.25 and ride the blue Downtown Shuttle the four blocks up to Anapamu Street. At 1114 State Street is La Arcada. From State Street, turn right onto Anapamu and on your right will be the Library, then cross Anacapa and turn right on it to see the Courthouse. After three blocks don't cross Canon Perdido, but turn left onto it and check out El Presidio State Historic Park. Turn right onto Santa Barbara Street and you've finished!

Exercise your creativity at Arts Alive!

Arts Alive!

Rating: A for locals, culture, diversity, and creativity
Ages: All
Directions: Call first
Contact: 963-2278 or www.artsalivesb.com
Season: Year-round

Tip: This is more for locals as it involves classes.

Arts Alive! offers more than 100 courses in ceramics, sculpture, painting, drawing, drumming, dancing, fabrics and costume design, sewing, music, songwriting and theatre arts, all under one roof! Intergenerational classes are offered on Saturdays, where children and adult teams create together. Home-school and pre-school programs allow students to work in a "real" studio environment. For teenagers, there is coursework in advanced level figure drawing, portfolio production, biographical writing, artwork documentation, art school investigation and gallery management. For adults, there are classes in areas of creativity which are not currently offered other places in our community. This is an amazing resource. Drop-ins are welcome.

Also see "Arts & Crafts Options" in Chapter 7, *Rainy/Dark/Cold: What To Do*.

Viewing with 3D glasses at Museum of Natural History.

Learn About Planets
Westmont and Museum of Natural History

Westmont College:
Rating: A for educational
Ages: 4-up
Directions: 101 South, exit Olive Mill Road in Montecito. Turn toward mountains and go about a mile to Hot Springs Road. Turn left onto Hot Springs, then 200 yards later turn right at the stop onto Sycamore Canyon. Stay on Sycamore Canyon about two miles and turn right onto Cold Springs Road to Westmont College on your left. It's about a mile up to Carroll Observatory.
Contact: 565-7040 or 565-6055
Season: Every third Friday of the month.

Tip: Call first and note 7:30 p.m. start time. Only go if it's clear weather! A public viewing of the stars is available.

Santa Barbara Museum of Natural History's "The Magic Sky"
Rating: A
Ages: 4-7
Directions: 101 North, exit Mission, turn towards mountains, go about two miles and after you pass the Mission on your left, follow the signs to take your first left to the parking lot, at 2559 Puesta Del Sol.
Contact: Museum 682-4711. Observatory 682-3224
Season: Saturdays at 11 a.m., year-round.

Tip: Call the observatory for events other than Saturdays. "The Magic Sky," about an hour long, is a great introduction to the planets for little ones.

Waterfowl abounds at Lake Los Carneros.

Lake Los Carneros

Rating: B- for not world class, but fresh air walk, wild birds, nature, peaceful
Ages: All ages, but it may be difficult for strollers to make it around the lake
Directions: 101 North, exit Los Carneros Road, turn right, pass Calle Real, and turn right at the county fire station on your right. Can also be accessed from Covington Way off Los Carneros Road or La Patera Lane off Calle Real
Contact: 568-2465 for group area reservations for a fee
Season: 8 a.m. to sunset

Tip: If you call 681-5514 and are lucky, you may get a Fire Station 14 tour! It's adjacent to Lake Los Carneros.

"La Patera" means "duck" in Spanish, so the lane bordering this is aptly named! This Santa Barbara County Park is an interesting jewel, which earns an "A" rating if combined with the South Coast Railroad Museum (964-3540), across the street from the fire station. Bring a picnic lunch or snack for the George Adams Picnic Grove tables. It's really a walking trail, as bikes and strollers have a hard time in parts. No swimming or boating. Feeding the ducks is like giving them candy; it's not good for their bodies and keeps them from hunting for their own healthy food. The only restroom is portable and is in the parking lot off Los Carneros Road. This educational outing can be five-hours long if combined with the museum and fire station! It's best with warmer weather, but try going early or late in the day when the light makes it even more beautiful!

Spring is when the plants are the greenest. The eucalyptus trees provide a Winter haven for monarch butterflies from January to February. Some might recommend steering clear of this lake during the evening hours due to the fact that the only way to catch the West Nile Virus is by being bitten by an infected mosquito – and mosquitos at the lake have tested positive for West Nile Virus.

Public marsh tours depart from Sandyland and Ash Saturdays at 10 a.m.

Conservation: UCSB Reserves

Rating: A for pristine, conservation, and educational
Ages: First grade to senior citizens
Directions: Contact reserve for directions before going
Contact: Director of each reserve for permission
Season: Reserve with Director Monday through Friday 9 a.m.-4 p.m.

Tip: It's worth the planning and organization.

Note: *These are extended teaching moments on biology, geography and the environment. California tax dollars pay for 35 reserves in the University of California system. Of those 35, eight are owned by UCSB and three are locally accessible. These are primarily research stations but available to the public for no charge periodically. There are 120 docents/volunteer guides. Educational groups are preferred. Visiting these reserves would be good prerequisites to going offshore to visit Channel Islands National Park.*

Carpinteria Salt Marsh Reserve: You've driven by it a zillion times but do you know its fascinating secrets or have you seen the sharks come in with the tide? Contact Dr. Andy Brooks, Director, at 893-7670 or go to: http://nrs.ucop.edu/reserves/carpinteria/carpinfo.html

Coal Oil Point Reserve: Out of the way, but a peaceful, beautiful jewel unknown to many. Walking completely around it is best, and maps are available from the director. Early or late, the light is best, but during midday it's warmer. You can start with a mini-beach day one-half mile past Coal Oil Point, at Sands Beach. Then turn inland after the snowy plover areas. If you have a group of little ones, once you return to the pavement, have an adult wait with the children and send drivers back for the cars. Contact Dr. Cristina Sandoval, Director, at 893-5092 or go to: http://coaloilpoint.ucnrs.org/subpage1/visitor/

Sedgwick Reserve: Francis and Alice Sedgwick gave these 6,000 acres to us. Deer, rabbits, squirrels, hawks, black bear, ticks, great blue heron, mountain lions, bobcats, rattlesnakes, chipmunks, gophers and rattlesnakes have been seen. It's too hot during summer. There is indoor accommodation (two rooms, four bunks in each) for eight. It's about a 50-minute drive. It was featured on the cover of the January 2006 Santa Barbara Seasons magazine. Contact Dr. Michael Williams, Director, at 686-1941 or http://nrs.ucop.edu/reserves/sedgwick/moreinfo.html.

The Carpinteria trolley is an easy one to four hours.

Carpinteria Trolley (MTD Seaside Shuttle)

Rating: A during warm weather; open-air, good view, cheap ride!
Ages: All
Directions: 101 South ten minutes, exit Linden Avenue. Turn right onto Linden, and park after the first signal. Look for trolley stops along Linden.
Contact: 963-3364 or www.sbmtd.gov
Season: Weekends approximately 8 a.m.-6 p.m. every 15 minutes, weekdays approximately 6 a.m.-6 p.m. every 30 minutes.

Tip: Bring a sweater; the open-air trolley may feel a little cool.

Bring your sense of adventure (and a picnic lunch) and get off at your whim! You can stop at El Carro Park (there's a playground), the beach, downtown (ice cream!), or Carpinteria Salt Marsh. Can be combined with a trip to see the harbor seal rookery east of the Venoco Pier just south/east of Carpinteria State Park December through May (seal pup birthing begins in February). The trolley is $0.25 per ride, even if you stay on the entire loop! Depending on your energy, interest and free time, this could be a five hour adventure. If you're going to the beach, bring a change of clothes.

Volunteering and caring for animals: a big lesson.

Dog Rental (Free)

Rating: A for community service, animal awareness, education
Ages: 5 and up; use your discretion
Directions: 5480 Overpass Road. 101 North, exit Patterson, turn toward the ocean, turn right on Overpass Road
Contact: 681-0561 or www.sbdawg.com
Season: You must go to Orientation one time for one hour, Saturdays at 2 p.m., prior to being able to walk dogs any time you like during their schedule. Hours are 10:00 am -5:00 pm Wednesday - Saturday, and 10:00 am -3:00 pm on Sunday. Other days and time by appointment.

Tip: Small children even with adults cannot actually hold the leash, but they sure can enjoy being with a dog!

This activity could change your life and your child's as well! The non-profit organization Dog Adoption & Welfare Group (D.A.W.G.) has a simple goal: keep dogs alive. It's owned and operated by volunteers. They know dogs well and can't afford to let a dog bite a child. They carefully screen which dogs should go out with whom. DAWG also provides healthcare, training and loving high-quality care for dogs that are lost or abandoned, so that they may be placed in a loving home. At least one human life has literally been saved by a dog coming out of this program. Volunteer – rent a dog for free – and take it for a walk. Community service is a wonderful thing for children of all ages to learn. Every child should do this at least once; it's priceless even if you already own a dog.

Jeanie Vaughan at Turtle Dreams welcomes volunteer groups.

Turtle Dreams

Rating: A for educational, community-mindedness, beyond fun
Ages: 4 and up
Directions: Call for group reservations/directions
Contact: Jeanie Vaughan, 969-4609 or fax 969-5128
Season: Year-round

Tip: Donate your group's time and money!

When Jeanie Vaughan was eight, she fell in love with turtles and tortoises and knew she wanted to spend her life taking care of them. This non-profit organization, started in 1995, on her property consists of Jeanie Vaughan and her daughter. They provide education about the conservation of turtles as well as rescue and rehabilitation. They accomplish this all on their own dime and by donations. She accepts only groups of visitors/volunteers. She has about 60 species of turtles including more than 500 of the shelled persuasion, some pig-nosed, some hinged, some box turtles, some smiling and some with "skirts." You can make this a teaching opportunity about community service. Your group can learn about turtles and then donate your time with something as simple as picking leaves off a plant for turtle food! She also has large iguanas, birds and frogs.

The Lizard's Mouth – up close and personal.

Lizard's Mouth

Rating: A+ for active, nature, educational and easy
Ages: 4 and up; use your discretion on hand-holding
Directions: 101 North, exit Highway 154. Before the top of the pass, turn left on West Camino Cielo. Go about 3 miles to where a small white vertical sign with three orange reflectors is on the left side of the road about six feet from a big outcrop of solid rock. This is the trailhead.
Season: Rain-free and fog-free days

Tip: Let an adult lead in case of rattlesnake sightings. Wear a Band-Aid over your ring so it won't get scratched. Bring water, a picnic lunch, and sunscreen or hats.

This is the best hike in the book for little ones to start with. The trailhead is easy to find, and the hike is a cake walk. If you miss the trailhead you'll end up at Santa Barbara Gun Club! Don't hike there! Turn around and head back east and you'll see the small sign next to a solid rock outcrop, across the road from an iron "No shooting" sign about 200 yards from the gun club. Follow the rock outcrop up and remember where you started. There is a dirt trail at the bottom left of the rock outcrop if you feel safer there. After about a five or 10-minute walk, towards the end of the rock outcrop, the trail veers off to the left. The actual "Lizard's Mouth" is between the far end of the rock outcrop and the Goleta-view rocks, a little hard to find. From the road it's about 20 minutes along the trail to a cool cave. Just past that, more rocks and mini-caves to climb on and in. On the back side of those rocks are great views of Goleta, Santa Barbara Channel, and the islands. The solid rock makes for great footing for little ones, and boy, do they love to climb!

Ropes courses offer a ton of activities.

Ropes Course (Adventure Challenge at UCSB)

Rating: A if you have a group!
Ages: First grade and up
Directions: Reserve first; they will provide directions.
Contact: 893-3737
Season: Ironically, more appointments are available during the school year

Tip: Remember, you must pay to park, so car pooling will save your group some money.

Groups of up to 15 cost approximately $300 and groups of up to 20 cost about $400 for three hours of climbing a 30' wall with a harness, a free-fall swing, a platform jump, zipline, group games on the ground, and an indoor course. It happens rain or shine. Tuesday and Thursday evenings 7:00-10:00 p.m., Friday and Saturday mornings 9:00 a.m.-Noon by appointment only.

A doll and teddy bear museum, right in Santa Barbara.

Susan Quinlan Doll & Teddy Bear Museum & Library

Rating: A for it's theme of "love of reading"
Ages: All
Directions: Inland on Garden Street to Canon Perdido, turn left to 122 West Canon Perdido.
Contact: 730-1707 or www.quinlanmuseum.com
Season: Open 11 am-5 pm Friday through Monday and many holidays

Tip: This is a great activity for Grandma and Grandpa!

There are more than 3,000 dolls and teddy bears here! Also enjoy the space toys, puppets, gift shop and tea room for complimentary coffee and tea.

Opened in 2005, this facility displays historical dolls, contemporary dolls and ethnic dolls.

Since it's handicapped accessible, grandmothers and grandfathers of all types can join in on the fun.

You know if you've already "Googled" for something like this, you have to drive a long way to find something comparable!

There are three galleries, and exhibits change periodically, so keep checking in to see what's new!

Hours of practice culminate in the Spirit of Fiesta auditions.

Spirit of Fiesta Auditions

Rating: A+
Ages: Those who can sit quietly and appreciate dance.
Directions: 101 South .05 mile, exit Milpas, left at the signal, turn left after one mile at Cota Street, to 721 E. Cota where there is a parking lot on the right. It's in Marjorie Luke Theatre inside Santa Barbara Junior High School.
Contact: 964-1590 or www.oldspanishdays-fiesta.org
Season: It's a Saturday one-day event and in years past it has been in March, April and May. In 2008 it was on April 5.

Tip: This is an all-day event.

Simply put, here are the best school-age dancers defining Santa Barbara, competing for the titles of "Spirit of Fiesta" and "Junior Spirit." The winners represent the City during Old Spanish Days.

As you know, Fiesta is a long and storied tradition in Santa Barbara, so this as competitive as any school sporting event. It's all about dance and presentation; everyone brings their own ability, style and attitude. The top competitors will amaze you. The youngest will astound you.

The hats and dresses are gorgeous and so distinctive. The composure of these solo contestants, in the spotlight, with everything on the line, is impressive.

It costs more than twice as much as going to see a movie, but it's three times the value. Where else can you see so many great young dancers that illustrate our City's culture and history?

In the spirit of inclusion, anyone can compete. Be prepared to see those who just want to go for it, even if it's the last thing they do. It's a long day inside a theatre, but you can attend until you've had your fill.

Finally, there is the crowning moment with all the emotion of a "Miss USA" pageant. This is truly one of the secrets of the Santa Barbarians; it's worth the effort of researching it, buying tickets and making room for it on your calendar.

There's plenty to see and do at the Wharf.

"Come Ye to the Waters"

Isaiah 55:1

Eliminate some things superfluous from your life. Break a habit. Do something that makes you feel insecure. *– Pierre Ferruci*

These shores supply waters to a thirsty soul! If there's a threat of nature-deficit disorder, the thrills of outdoor nature play are right in front of you. Try simply going to the beach, pedal boats, the fishermen's market, Lil' Toot the Water Taxi, tide pooling, whale watching, fishing, surfing, sailing or beachcombing.

Let the moment unfold and your children will find freedom, fantasy, privacy and peace – all on their own. Let them create their own experience and feel their senses broaden with more of their lives spent in the natural world. They'll expand their boundaries, take more risks and gain greater confidence.

If you're taking a young one, use your discretion to determine which activity is appropriate for your child. You know your child best. The Coast Guard requires that all children under 13 years of age wear Coast Guard-approved life jackets while aboard recreational vessels underway.

Viva la agua!

The twin-hull Condor Express departs for whale watching.

Whale Watching & Big Boat Trips

Rating: A+ for educational, boating, family
Ages: Use your discretion; you know your child best
Season: Gray whales December to April. Blue whales June to August. More than 28 species of whales and porpoises pass through the channel. It's better weather and there is less swell during the warmer months.

> **Tip:** To avoid heavy seas, ask a surf shop if there is a big swell running.

See majestic gray whales as they migrate south to mate in Mexico. Since the channel waters are protected, it makes for one of the finest whale-watching areas in the world.

- **Captain Don's Whale Watching Tours:** 969-5217 or www.captdon.com, it's out on Stearns Wharf. Captain Don's boat, the *Rachel* G, is offering whale-watching, pirate cruises and sunset cruises. It is a 149-passenger Power Yacht. Board at Stearns Wharf at State and Cabrillo.

Harbor Directions: 101 North 0.5 mile, exit Bath Street (Castillo), turn left at the signal (Haley St.), then left again at the next signal onto Castillo Street. Go 0.4 to the T intersection of Castillo and Cabrillo/Shoreline, and turn right onto Shoreline Drive. Take your first left into Santa Barbara Harbor parking lot.

- **Condor Cruises:** 564-6750 or www.condorcruises.com. The 145-passenger twin-hulled boat also offers trips out to the Channel Islands from adjacent launch ramp.
- **Sunset Kidd Sailing Charters**, 962-8222 or www.sunsetkidd.com. If you prefer to sail while whale watching, or want a sunset sail, this 41-foot Morgan Out Island ketch carries a maximum of 18 passengers.
- **Double Dolphin**, 962-2826, or www.sbsail.com. Adjacent to the launch ramp, this 50-foot sailing catamaran operated by Santa Barbara Sailing Center has 1,400-square-feet of deck space and can accommodate 49 passengers.

"Surf Central" is at Leadbetter Beach when the surf is up.

Best Beaches

※ **Leadbetter Beach** is the place to go to watch surfers, at low tide. There is a grassy area, picnic tables and a restroom. The cliffs partially block the prevailing northwest winds, and there's plenty of pay parking. Palm trees line the beach and there is a Cypress tree at the point. This is one of Santa Barbara's most popular beaches. Shoreline Grill allows you to dine sitting at a table with your toes in the sand! Directions: 101 north 0.5 mile, exit Bath Street (Castillo), turn left at the signal then left again at the next signal, onto Castillo street. Go 0.4 mile to the T intersection of Castillo and Cabrillo/Shoreline, and turn right onto Shoreline Drive. Take your second left (Loma Alta Drive), into the parking lot, then turn right toward the kiosk.

※ **Sand Spit Beach** is where you can be standing at the beach and be facing east viewing the mountains as boats enter and leave the harbor. This gem is rarely visited. It's a 20-minute walk, but worth it. Facing the ocean, you can watch the sunrise, or have the sun at your back at sunset! No restroom. Directions: 101 north 0.5 mile, exit Bath Street (Castillo), turn left at the signal then left again at the next signal, onto Castillo street. Go 0.4 mile to the T intersection of Castillo and Cabrillo/Shoreline, and turn right onto Shoreline Drive. Take your first left, into the parking lot, and park. Walk out the breakwater, then along the tiny path along/atop the jetty rocks.

※ **East Beach** means volleyball courts, huge stretches of sand, playground equipment on the sand, restrooms, and East Beach Grill for breakfast and lunch. Directions: From Garden Street, go toward the water then turn left onto Cabrillo for one mile.

※ **Butterfly Beach** in Montecito almost disappears at high tide, and is where monarch butterflies sometimes winter. There are no restrooms, parking places are free, but scarce on hot days. The sand seems finer, and the waves seem smaller on this quiet beach. Directions: 101 South three miles, exit Olive Mill, turn right at the stop and go 0.5 mile. South Butterfly is more for the Four Seasons Resort guests; North Butterfly is more for locals.

※ **Hendry's Beach**, adjacent to Hope Ranch, has surfing waves, cliffs, Rusty Pelican Restaurant, restrooms and free parking. A popular beach with locals. Directions: 101 North three miles, exit Las Positas, turn left at the light all the way to Cliff Drive. Turn right and then left into the parking lot.

Andree Clark Bird Refuge is ideal for birdwatching.

Andree Clark Bird Refuge

Rating: A for beauty, quiet moments and wildlife up-close-and-personal
Ages: Toddlers to 100
Directions: 101 South, exit Cabrillo Blvd. to the right, and 200' after passing under the railroad bridge, turn right into the parking lot at 1400 E. Cabrillo Blvd.
Contact: This is as outdoors as outdoors gets!
Season: Winter boasts more migrating birds, summer is warmer!

Tip: Don't feed the birds. Bring your bikes/bike locks and binoculars. After birdwatching, take your bike on the bike path along Cabrillo Boulevard. Use your discretion as to how far your child can bike!

This 29-acre fresh-brackish water lake and marsh pond is adjacent to the zoo. It began as a salt marsh fed by Sycamore Creek, but the construction of the railroad in the 1880s isolated it. It is named after the sister of Huguette M. Clark, Andree Clark. In 1928 Huguette donated the property to the City with the requirement that it be maintained indefinitely as a 42-acre bird refuge.

Walk west up the trail to visit three viewing platforms on the north side of the lake. Try for quiet moments listening and watching.

Then put your binoculars back in the car and hit the bike trail along Cabrillo Boulevard. Follow the bike path along the lake to the second signal light, walk your bike across Cabrillo Boulevard and take the bike path along the sand, passing or stopping along the way at Skater's Point skateboard park, the Sunday arts and crafts show, Stearns Wharf, the wading pool/playground, the Harbor, West Beach, Leadbetter Beach, and Shoreline Park. It's flat except for the 200 yards up to Shoreline Park, where there is playground equipment, if you've made it that far. You've just biked 3.9 miles; ready to go back? (Remember to turn back when you are HALF-way tired!) Sometimes you can see whales migrating December-April. There are ice cream, snacks and restaurants at the wharf and harbor.

Stearns Wharf Bait & Tackle rents poles.

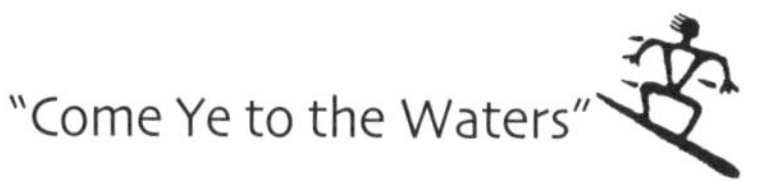

Something Fishy

Rating: You make the call!
Ages: Use your discretion since you know your child best
Directions: See below
Contact: See below

Tip: Rent equipment and follow The Bait Shop advice on best bait. Make reservations before going to the boat.

- **Stearns Wharf** At the foot of State Street, Stearns Wharf Bait & Tackle, 965-1333, is located on the pier, but there is no railing; it's not ideal for young children. Rental poles and reels are available. Buy a crab trap and drop it for a potpourri sampling of the ocean floor!
- **Goleta Pier** Take 101 North 10 minutes, exit Highway 217, exit Sandspit Road, turn left to Goleta Beach Park. There is no bait and tackle shop.
- **Sea Landing** quarter-day, half-day, full-day, and multi-day trips aboard the 75 foot high-speed catamaran sportfishing boat Condor Express at the harbor launch ramp, 963-3564 or www.patriotsportfishing.com. Truth Aquatics is the official concessionaire in Santa Barbara of Channel Islands National Park, offering whale watching, dinner cruises, scuba trips and Channel Island trips at www.condorcruises.com.
- **Wavewalker Charters** sportfishing for six people at 964-2046

Once you're "stoked," you can't put it down.

"Let's Go Surfin' Now…"

Rating: Depends on waves/instructor/water temp/wetsuit/board
Ages: 9 and up is best, but some children take to it earlier; use your discretion
Directions: Call
Contact: Compare rates (private about $45.00/hr.) and group surf lesson offers below
Season: Surf is bigger in winter. If Santa Barbara is dead flat, there may be waves to ride 20 minutes away.

Tip: A wetsuit (personal or rented) and at least one surf lesson are strongly recommended. Lessons include a wetsuit and board, and make it safer and more fun. If you must skip lessons, drive to A-Frame Surf Shop where they have boards, wetsuits, and (most likely of all area beaches) waves all in one place. Humbly ask a surfer on the beach for some tips beforehand, if you can't afford a lesson. Listen as long as he/she will talk.

For surf instruction:

※ **A-Frame Surf Shop,** 684-8803; 101 South 10 minutes to Santa Claus Lane exit, continue straight at the stop to 3785 Santa Claus Lane. This surf shop is run by two friendly and enthusiastic brothers, Rob and Sam Holcombe. The white sand beach here can have ridable waves when Santa Barbara is flat. Private lesson for $55.00 includes board, wetsuit, 1.5 hours instruction, and 1-2 hours of board and wetsuit rental after the lesson.

※ **Santa Barbara Seals Surf School** 687-9785 or www.santabarbara seals.com Location depends on the surf, and also offers after-school surf programs.

※ **Santa Barbara Adventure Company** 898-0671 or www.sb adventureco.com also offers paragliding, kayaking and mountain climbing adventures

※ **Santa Barbara Surf School** 745-8877 or www.santabarbarasurf school. com offers instruction including private lessons for about $95.00 for two hours including wetsuit and board, and day camps all year long

※ **Surf Country Surf Shop** 683-4450 or www.surfcountry.net. Take 101 North 9 minutes to Patterson exit, turn right at signal then immediately left onto Calle Real to 5668 in Goleta, if you're based north of Santa Barbara

※ **Surf Happens** 966-3613 or www.surfhappens.com Ex-professional surfer Chris Keet founded the Santa Barbara Surfing Association, and founded Surf Happens in 2000. He continually gives back to the sport and his summer camp is always in high demand!

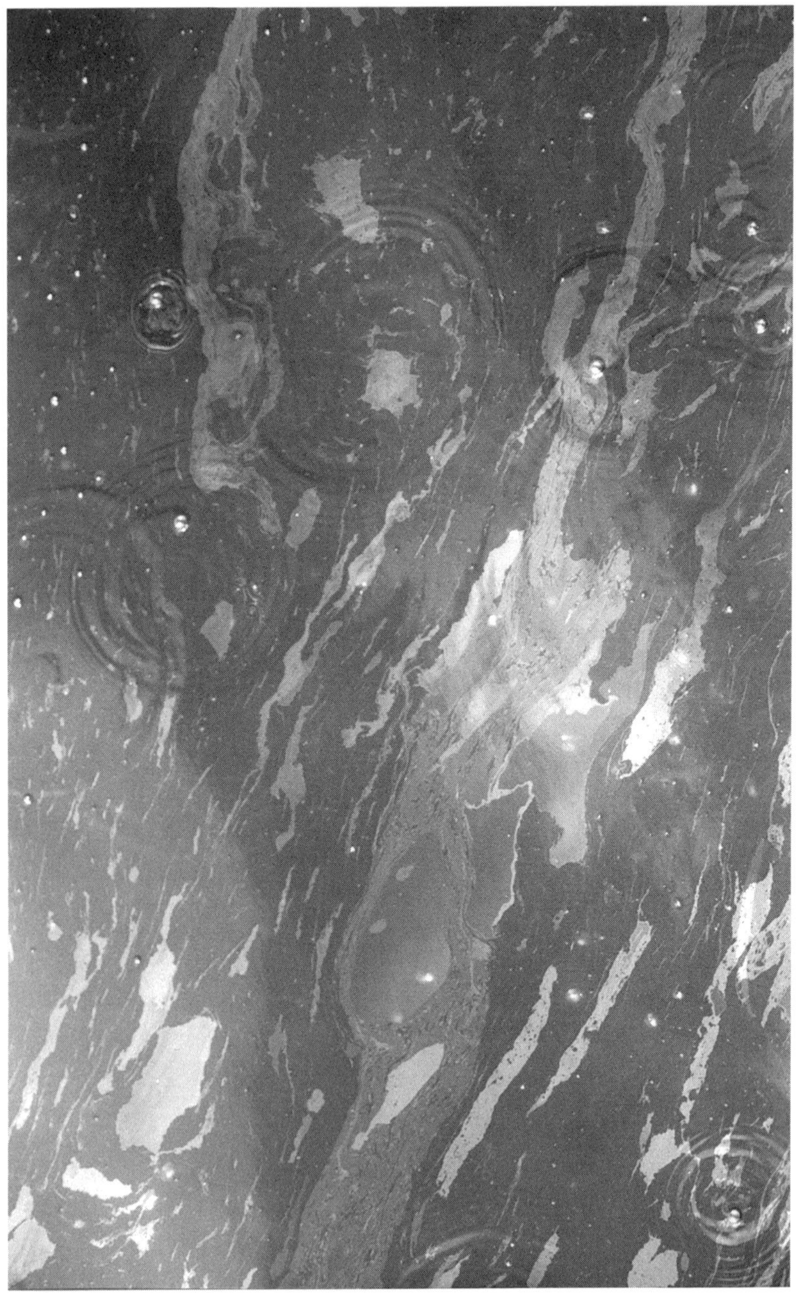

Oil makes patterns on the ocean water at the seep.

Oil Seep Tour

Rating: A for quick, educational, boat ride, offshore!
Ages: Use your own discretion
Directions: 101 North 0.5 mile, exit Bath Street (Castillo), turn left at the signal (Haley St.), then left again at the next signal onto Castillo Street. Go 0.4 to the T intersection of Castillo and Cabrillo/Shoreline, and turn right onto Shoreline Drive. Take your first left into Santa Barbara Harbor parking lot.
Contact: www.venocoinc.com to check the schedule or Sea Landing at 882-0088
Season: 1.5-hour tours on weekends, May through September

Tip: Call 882-0088 for reservations, prices and directions.

Many believe that tar on the beaches is a result of oil companies drilling offshore, but Chumash people of the past used beach tar to caulk their *tomols* (canoes) years before the first oil derrick ever appeared in the channel. Venoco Oil Company gives the general public a view of the "World's Most Spectacular Seeps" near Coal Oil Point aboard the *Condor Express*, departing from the Sea Landing dock in the harbor. About 6,000 gallons of oil seeps naturally from the ocean floor each day, and about five million cubic feet of natural gas rises from the ocean floor each day. After the seeps, the boat goes near *Platform Holly* and the tour guide explains how it operates. The captain of the boat points out marine mammals along the way. This tour may change your thoughts about tar, oil derricks and oil companies, especially if you drive to the harbor in a car!

Tidepools at Devereux/Coal Oil Point include crabs.

Tidepooling

Rating: A for education/nature/family
Ages: Use your discretion! Hold hands to avoid slipping on rocks.
Directions: See below
Contact: None
Season: The best time to go is usually in autumn or winter afternoons

Tip: Check the daily paper for low tides. 0.0 or minus tides are best! Keep no live organisms! If the surf is up, beware of sudden waves on incoming tides.

- **Carpinteria State Beach** 101 South, 10 minutes, exit Casitas Pass Road, right on Casitas Pass, right on Carpinteria Avenue, left on Palm, pay to enter, then go to the southernmost parking lot. Easily combined with sea lion viewing – just a 10-minute walk south.
- **Leadbetter Beach** 101 North, exit Bath/Castillo, left on Haley, left at Castillo. Go under the freeway and when you hit Cabrillo Boulevard, turn right. Left at your second signal into the pay parking lot for Leadbetter Beach. Centrally located, more crowded.
- **Goleta Point** 101 North 10 minutes, exit Highway 217 to UCSB, turn left at UCSB onto Lagoon Road, then take your next left into Parking Lot #6 and purchase a parking ticket at the machine. The Point sticks out into the Santa Barbara Channel more than any other around. More of a country feel.
- **Coal Oil Point Reserve** 101 North, 10 minutes, exit Los Carneros, turn left. When it hits El Colegio Road, turn right. Then take your second left (Camino Corto). When it hits Del Playa, turn right. Go to the end and park free. Easy access down the cliff here, then walk along the beach west to the point. Most country feel, and this reserve is managed by UCSB.

Tandem kayaks go anywhere in Santa Barbara County!

Kayaking (water fun and barely getting wet!)

Rating: A for active, family, educational, aesthetic
Ages: Use a tandem kayak, and use your discretion
Directions: 101 North 0.5 mile, exit Bath Street (Castillo), turn left at the signal (Haley St.), then left again at the next signal onto Castillo Street. Go 0.4 to the T intersection of Castillo and Cabrillo/Shoreline, and turn right onto Shoreline Drive. Take your first left into Santa Barbara Harbor parking lot.

Tip: Use a life vest for you and your little one and share a tandem kayak; they don't even have to paddle . . . you can paddle and guide it the whole time until they're able. Dress in layers so you're the right temperature, since it's cooler on the water.

- **Paddle Sports of Santa Barbara**, 899-4925, www.kayaksb.com, and
- **Santa Barbara Sailing Center**, 962-2826, www.sbsail.com, are both at the harbor. Great if you want to paddle around the harbor (don't worry about boats in this tiny harbor) or along the coast, or take a trip with others. After you feel the harbor is no longer a challenge, paddle under the wharf or out to the green buoy to see sea lions on top! If you're a beginner to advanced, and want instruction or a guided tour to kayak the coastline or Channel Islands, home to one of the biggest sea caves in the world, no problem! Contact Paddle Sports above or
- **Aquasports/Ocean Kayak Adventures** at 968-7231 www.island kayaking.com
- **Santa Barbara Adventure Company** (888) 773-3239 or 898-0671 www.sbadventureco.com

Sailing gives you a new perspective.

Sailboat Cruises & Rentals, Motorized Watercraft

Rating: A for fresh air and wonderful view
Ages: Swimmers and up
Directions: 101 North 0.5 mile, exit Bath Street (Castillo), turn left at the signal (Haley St.), then left again at the next signal onto Castillo Street. Go 0.4 to the T intersection of Castillo and Cabrillo/Shoreline, and turn right onto Shoreline Drive. Take your first left into Santa Barbara Harbor parking lot.
Season: Depends on what you're looking for!

Tip: Dress in layers as it's cooler on the water.

- **Do It Yourselfers Santa Barbara Sailing Center**, 962-2826, www.sbsail.com. About 600 feet past the parking kiosk is the launch ramp and the Santa Barbara Sailing Center floating to the right of it. If you must steer yourself, there are more than 20 sailboats and motorboats to rent, some less than 17 feet long. Paddle boats and single and tandem kayaks are also available to rent at this professional, well-run operation that has reasonable rates.
- **Double-Dolphin** 962-2826 or www.sbsail.com. A wonderful 50' sailing catamaran, offers coastal sails and cruises for up to 49 passengers. You want to bring a cooperative child to enjoy sunsets, mountain views, shoreline views and possible sea creatures. Voted First Place *Sunset Cruise Boat* by the readers of *The Independent*. If you'd like to have a yacht and captain all to yourself for a custom-made few days at the islands, contact this company for Charter Cruises. It's the best-spent money possible!
- **Sunset Kidd** 962-8222 or www.sunsetkidd.com. A classic monohull 41' Morgan Out Island Ketch, takes a maximum of 18 passengers on morning, afternoon and sunset cruises, as well as whale watching. It boards right near the parking kiosk at the harbor.
- **Personal Water Craft** (PWC) 963-3564 or www.sealanding.net. You'll never see anyone in a bad mood on a PWC. Up to three people can ride one. Called Wave Runners or Sea-Doos, they're like motorcycles on water. Best on warmer days or with a wetsuit as you may fall off and get wet, but you climb back on and that's part of the fun!

Whether fast or slow, it's good to be on the water.

Water Sports (Sea Landing)

Rating: A+ If you can't find something here, you don't like water
Ages: Swimmers/use your knowledge of your child
Directions: 101 North 0.5 mile, exit Bath Street (Castillo), turn left at the signal (Haley St.), then left again at the next signal onto Castillo Street. Go 0.4 to the T intersection of Castillo and Cabrillo/Shoreline, and turn right onto Shoreline Drive. Take your first left into Santa Barbara Harbor parking lot.
Contact: 963-3564 or www.sealanding.net
Season: The warmer, the better. However, if you dress properly, it can be great in the winter.

Tip: Call for information about current activities. You might find yourself in a whale watching boat or personal watercraft (PWC).

At the harbor, you can find more activities per square foot than anywhere in Santa Barbara. Depart for whale watching, deep-sea fishing, scuba trips, or Channel Island trips. You can rent a small jet boat, sailboat, kayak, or personal watercraft (PWC), often called Wave Runners. Life vests are always included, and wetsuits are often included. If you're hungry after your activity, you have several restaurants to choose from at the harbor village, and two more on Stearns Wharf – a short Lil' Toot water-taxi ride away.

Everyone can find a rental bike style they like.

Surreys, Bicycles and Other Cycles

Rating: A for healthy, outside, and family-oriented
Ages: Anyone who can hang on!
Directions: Cabrillo Boulevard from Andree Clark Bird Refuge to Shoreline Park is the bike trail, and it's all flat until you head past Leadbetter Beach. Start anywhere or rent bikes/surreys and other wheeled vehicles.

Wheel Fun Rentals, 23 E. Cabrillo Blvd., 633 E. Cabrillo, 1111 E. Cabrillo Blvd., 966-2282 or www.wheelfunrentals.com
Open Air Bicycles, 224 Chapala St., 963-3717 or www.openairbicycles.com

It's impossible to ride one of these *without* a smile on your face! Unfortunately, with all of the cycle companies, you have to cross busy Cabrillo Boulevard, but walking your cycle across the street on a green light sets a good example. Bring a bike lock if you want to make a day of it and lock it up somewhere during a break. You may run across a sandcastle building contest or who knows what! On busy summer days, they sell out. You've got to have a sense of humor and/or a sense of adventure; there's some type of rental for everyone. The biggest surreys have three rows plus a front basket seat for little ones; they're capable of carrying 11 riders! If you have your own bike, start at Andree Clark Bird Refuge, take your time and enjoy breaks at East Beach Grill (across from Hotel Mar Monte), Skater's Point skateboard park, the Wharf, Harbor Village, Shoreline Grill, or Leadbetter Beach. Ensure little ones stay on the right side of the bike path, and beware of crowded holiday weekends.

Rocky Nook Park's mosaic alligators are near the Mission Canyon Road bridge.

NOT Just a Park

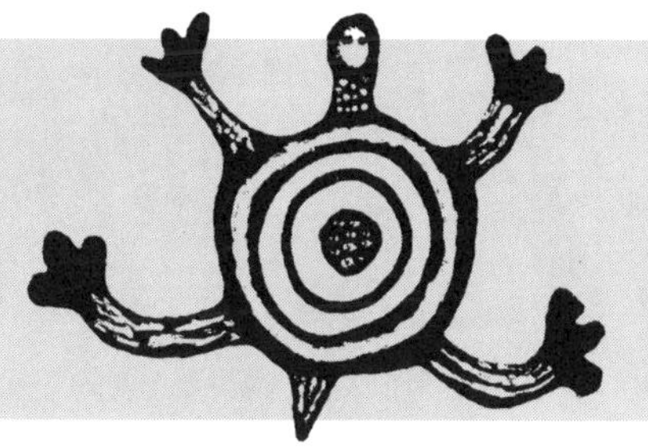

In all things of nature, there is something of the marvelous.
– Aristotle

Would anyone like to play in arguably the biggest fort in the world made by children? Can you imagine a 75-year-old toy still working? How would you like to feed a shark? How about an 1890's stagecoach stop with a rope swing over a creek? Have you seen the two mosaic alligators in the creek at Rocky Nook Park?

Santa Barbara offers a 1929 carousel at Chase Palm Park, an oceanfront skateboard park, urban "pocket" parks, and El Presidio State Historic Park. There are preserves with minimal man-made structures.

If you want to take your dog with you, off-leash, it's Douglas Family Preserve for you. It's completely undeveloped with cliff-top ocean views.

The parks herein have something special about them; they're not just a park . . .

Chase Palm Park Carousel: the best five minutes in town.

Chase Palm Park & Carousel

Rating: A+ for carousel, playground, bike path
Ages: All ages
Directions: 101, exit Garden Street, turn toward the beach, turn right into the pay parking lot after the railroad tracks, or continue past Cabrillo into the other pay parking lot. It's at the corner of Cabrillo Boulevard and Garden.
Contact: 564-5418. Office hours: 8-5 Monday through Friday
Season: Any dry day.

Tip: During the summer, there are open-air concerts at 5:30 p.m. on Thursdays; bring dinner, sand chairs and a blanket to the east end of the park. Visit the Visitors Center at 1 Garden Street if you need more information.

Pearl Chase and her brother, Harold, for whom this park is named, played major roles in shaping the Santa Barbara community from the time she graduated from college in 1909 until she passed in 1979. She focused her efforts on historic preservation, conservation and community development. Look for the bas relief sculpture plaque of Pearl and Harold. The park was expanded in 1998 when Fess Parker ("Daniel Boone" actor and owner of adjacent Fess Parker's DoubleTree Resort) donated the property on the inland side of the boulevard.

The Allan Herschel 1917 three-row portable carousel (10-6 daily) is top quality. There is a fountain and shipwreck playground, and adjacent (concrete) whales appear to be surfacing out of the sea (grass). You can check out toys at the office near the playground with a driver's license. There is a snack bar, and across the street is the waterfront Chase Palm Park and bike path. Below its palm trees on Saturdays at 4 p.m. there is a drum circle for anyone who has a drum or is interested in listening/drumming/dancing to drums. Fantastic!

Young and old grab their board and go sidewalk surfing.

Skateboard Park (Skater's Point)

Rating: A for spectator viewing – 20-30 minutes
Ages: Small children to seniors are spellbound watching these athletes.
Directions: 101 exit Garden Street. Turn toward the ocean. Go straight and you'll drive right across Cabrillo Boulevard and into the parking lot.
Contact: No contact on site. 897-2650 or 564-5418
Season: Sunrise to sunset any dry day.

Tip: Don't take your children here if you prefer they never take up skateboarding! Go off-hours if you're a beginner.

The Surgeon General has determined that skateboarding can be hazardous to your health. 'Nuff said. "Skateboarding is not a crime," the bumper stickers read.

Every minute of every dry day, it's show time and someone is on stage. Little children come here early, and there is an annual competition. Big kids, some tattooed and scary-looking, look out for and encourage little ones and beginners. The park is patrolled to encourage safety and the wearing of protective gear, discourage graffiti writers, bike riders and other rough stuff. For the quality of entertainment and high athletic skills exhibited, it's surprising there aren't bleachers here that are packed every day. It's mostly a participatory sport, but makes a great spectator sport too!

Exploring the big rock at Toro Canyon Park.

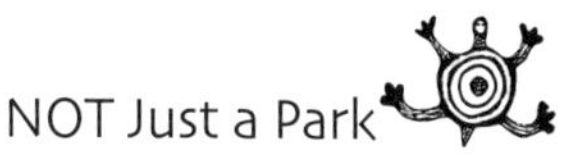

Toro Canyon Park

Rating: A for rock climbing, playgrounds, polliwogs, hiking
Ages: Toddler to Adult
Directions: 101 South 3 miles, exit Sheffield Drive. At stop turn toward mountains, the only way you can go. At next stop, turn right onto North Jameson. This will immediately curve left into Sheffield Dr. (do not turn right and go up Ortega Hill Rd.). At the top of Sheffield Dr. at the stop, turn right onto East Valley Rd. Go several miles until you see signs for Toro Canyon Park.
Contact: 969-3315
Season: Any dry day. The climate is different up here. It can be much warmer than anywhere in the flatlands!

Tip: Bring a picnic lunch and good walking shoes and drive to the farthest end of the parking lot. Explore the big rock on the other side of the creek if you're adventurous. Look south and you can see a gazebo 0.5 miles away uphill. Great view from up there. This place is magic, and quiet!

Nestled is the word for this park. It's tucked away, way back in there. Don't be limited by the playground equipment – walk beyond it, and you'll discover a wonderland of rocks, just waiting for climbers of all ages. Explore the creek and look for bugs. Think outside the box at this park, but watch for poison oak if you get in the brush. Real go-getters will hike to the Gazebo and see the ocean view to the south! This is a locals' favorite.

Upper Manning Park has paths, playgrounds, and tennis.

Manning Park

Rating: A for narrow paved trails, playgrounds, tennis
Ages: Toddler to adult
Directions: 101 South, exit San Ysidro Road. At stop sign, turn toward mountains. Just past Montecito Union School and Schoolhouse Road, turn left into upper Manning Park.
Contact: 568-2461, 969-0201or www.sbparks.org
Season: Daily 8 a.m. to sunset

Tip: Great on windy days since all the trees block the wind, and you can find a warm spot. Bring a picnic lunch. After a rain, there will be water in the creek that runs through the park! Afterward, drive 200 yards towards the mountains and turn right into Montecito Village for an ice cream treat at Pierre LaFond.

Playground, horseshoes, and tennis courts at upper Manning. "Beach" volleyball and playground equipment at Lower Manning down San Ysidro 300' and left at Santa Rosa, then left again into Lower Manning. Fantastic maze of paved trails and bridges to explore at Upper Manning. Great for a game of "Capture The Flag." Upper Manning Park may not have a playground as big as lower Manning, but for those with imagination, Upper Manning is a great place to play and explore. Just turn your 3- to 5-year-old loose and follow. Adventurous? Go across San Ysidro to the Lower Manning creek bed and look for polliwogs.

Beginners rock-hop at Rocky Nook Park

Rocky Nook

Rating: B+ for lots of variety; not your average grassy park
Ages: 2 to adult
Directions: 101 North, exit Mission Street. Turn right at the signal onto Mission. Stay on it to the end. At the T-intersection and stop sign at the end, turn left. Turn right at the next stop sign. After you pass the Mission and a stone bridge, turn right into Rocky Nook Park, on your right.
Contact: 681-5650 for group area reservations
Season: It's always several degrees warmer here than the temperature at the beach. Spring, fall and winter are ideal. In summer it's best to go early or late to avoid the heat of the day. Hours are 8 a.m. until sunset.

Tip: If you rock-hop in the creek stay away from dark or green rocks; they're slippery!

This playground is a nice one, and nearby are child-size boulders to practice climbing on. The adventurous might walk to the top of the park; take the trail down into Mission Creek when there isn't much water, and rock-hop downstream. Look for the rock painted like a frog, and farther downstream, look out for the life-sized mosaic alligators on the left bank before the bridge! Go under the bridge and you can make it all the way to the Museum of Natural History. Walk out of the creek on your left after you go under the footbridge. Watch out for poison oak.

Refugio State Beach on a good day is like Hawaii.

Refugio State Beach

Rating: A for prettiest beach in the area
Ages: All
Directions: 101 North 22 miles, exit Refugio Road, follow signs
Contact: www.parks.ca.gov or www.reserveamerica. com to reserve a camp spot or 968-1033 for current conditions
Season: Any

Tip: Go toward the farthest west tables or beach area for less wind.

The train goes very near this campground, like many others, but it's the palm trees, white sand, and surfers that make this place look like Hawaii. Kayaking is popular fun at this beach, but it's strictly bring your own. When there are no waves, you can snorkel the point/reef if you have a wetsuit, if it's late summer, or if you're a polar bear. You can take bikes to this park and pedal 2.5 miles to El Capitan State Beach. It's best to start at El Capitan State Beach and first pedal west to Refugio, then pedal east to El Capitan since the afternoon winds will be at your back as you return, and it will be easier.

Alice Keck Park Memorial Gardens has turtles.

Alice Keck Park Memorial Gardens

Rating: A+ for many children's favorite park in Santa Barbara
Ages: Toddler to adult
Directions: 1500 block of Santa Barbara Street
Contact: None
Season: It changes with every season, so go often

Tip: Research and plans are under way in order to reintroduce koi into the pond.

"Turtle Park," "Alice Keck Park Park," whatever you want to call it, this is a magic place if you have an imagination. Check out the little spring, and the touch garden for those who are unsighted. Sure, check out turtles and ducks, but get away from the main thoroughfares too. Steal a quiet moment. And don't forget Kids' World across Micheltorena Street. The variety of flora is amazing, and changes with the seasons.

Once the site of the elegant El Mirasol Hotel, this downtown block is often called the "crown jewel" of city parks. The park features a large botanical collection (75 different tree and plant species), sensory garden with audio posts and interpretive Braille signs, low water-using demonstration garden, picnic areas and a gazebo. There are reservable wedding and party sites.

Up close and personal with Franceschi's face.

Franceschi Park

Rating: A for best view in City Limits
Ages: 5 and up if you're quiet or imaginative
Directions: 101 North 2 miles, exit Mission Street toward the mountains, just past the Mission veer right up Alameda Padre Serra.Turn left at the stop sign at Moreno. Go 100 feet and veer right onto San Carlos. Turn right onto Mission Ridge. Turn left into the park, 1510 Mission Ridge Road.
Contact: 564-5418 for reservable picnic site
Season: The clearer the better, 8 a.m. to sunset

Tip: Walk down the trail at the far end of the parking lot until you find the three-foot-high sculpture of Franceschi's head overlooking the City!

This park and its exotic plants and home are named after previous owner, Italian horticulturist Francesco Franceschi. The best thing about this park is its drop-dead gorgeous view of the city, harbor, Mesa, Channel and islands. It encompasses 18 acres, an exceptional botanical collection, and the interesting, but dilapidated home of Franceschi. Most people come for the view, but it's great to look around, too. With no need for playground equipment, there are small trails to explore, perfect for little explorers. This place amazingly doesn't get crowded. Check out the plaques and reliefs near the driveway down below, and on the house, too. Look for his sculpture down the trail.

Two rope swings delight Arroyo Hondo visitors.

Arroyo Hondo Preserve

Rating: A for so distinct it was noted in 1542 in the logbook of Juan Rodriguez Cabrillo!
Ages: Toddler and up
Directions: Do not show up unless you have made a reservation.
Contact: 567-1115 or www.sblandtrust.org
Season: Open only the first and third weekends of the month, 10 a.m.-3 p.m. Reservations are required and include a docent-led tour. Closed on rainy days. The Ortega Adobe is only open noon to 1 p.m.

Tip: Reservations are required. Even if you don't last long on the tour with your little one, it's fascinating while it lasts. Take the trail up the canyon to the rope swings over the creek! Bring a picnic lunch.

This is the jewel in the crown of the Gaviota Coast. This 782-acre preserve is pristine. The area is rich in early California history, first as a Chumash village and later as a cattle ranch. It was purchased from the Hollister family (Hollister Avenue, Hollister Ranch) in 2001. The preserve features a beautiful sandy beach that's difficult to swim in because of the rocks. There are hiking trails, two rope swings over the creek, antique carriage outside the main house and beautiful plants. The 2004 fire came very close to the property but firefighters saved Arroyo Hondo.

The adobe house was built in 1842 by the Ortega family and was used as a stagecoach stop on the route between Lompoc and Santa Barbara during the late 1800s. The canyon was also known to be a refuge for infamous outlaws such as Joaquin Murrieta, Jack Powers and Judge Edward McGowan. You can almost picture them hiding out, partway up the east hill of the canyon where there is a flat area, above the meadow.

Members of the Santa Barbara Land Trust can camp at Arroyo Hondo once a year, an epic experience which includes a campfire talk on astronomy, wildlife and Sasquatch!

Douglas Family Preserve's off-leash dog policy is popular with many.

Douglas Family Preserve

Rating: A for fresh sea air, great views, a good walk
Ages: Toddlers up
Directions: 101 North, exit Carrillo, left at signal up and over the hill. Right at the Cliff Drive signal, then after Cooper Road, take the next left onto Mesa Lane. Turn right onto Medcliff Road and take it to the end and park. The preserve is adjacent to the neighborhood, skirting the cliff about 1/2 mile and the trail makes an oval if you stay on it.
Contact: www.santabarbara.com/activities/parks/douglas_family_preserve/
Season: Any time except when it's raining.

Tip: There are no restrooms. Keep your little one away from the cliff.

Here is undeveloped wide-open space sitting atop cliffs overlooking the Pacific Ocean. Dogs are allowed to run free. This place is simple: just clean air, Santa Barbara Channel views, and a pleasant walk. Once slated for development, locals rallied to buy the property. When prospects looked dim, Montecito resident Michael Douglas, son of actor Kirk Douglas, donated a large sum at the last minute to preserve the land as open space. It's especially wonderful for dog owners. If you, or your child, are not tolerant of dogs, walk the cliffs of More Mesa (Trail Mix chapter). It's not a good place to picnic – and people should watch where they step – between dog droppings and holes in the dirt from fallen eucalyptus tree trunks. There are trees, and fallen trees, which offer great climbing for children.

The 70-acre grassy preserve is on a 150-foot mesa with more than 2,000 feet of undeveloped ocean frontage. There are cypress, oak and eucalyptus trees, and below is Arroyo Burro Beach, also known to locals as Hendry's Beach.

Elings Park has a two-story play structure.

Elings Park

Rating: A for most abundant and diverse activities in Santa Barbara!
Ages: Toddlers and up
Directions: Take 101 North, exit Las Positas Road. Turn left at the signal, and go about one mile. Elings Park entrance is on the left.
Contact: 569-5611 or www.elingspark.org
Season: Whenever it is park weather or you feel motivated!

Tip: Do yourself a favor and visit the Web site on this one. There are so many things this park offers!

Elings Park has something for everyone. It has summer camps and day camps. There are programs in softball, soccer, baseball, BMX bicycle racing, remote control car racing, paragliding instruction, hang gliding instruction, art, Tae Kwon Do, and Shakespeare characters. It has an off-leash dog program for an annual fee. There are overnight family camping nights during the summer. There are Family Movie nights. There are bike festivals, dog shows, car shows and barbeques. This park is of enormous benefit to the community.

Elings Park is unique because it is built on land reclaimed from the old city landfill, and is owned and administered by a non-profit organization.

It even has a serious mountain-bike trail!

The area's shortest trail shows ancient Chumash art.

Chumash Painted Cave State Historic Park

Rating: A for culture and rock hopping nearby
Ages: The older the better to appreciate the rock art
Directions: 101 North, exit Highway 154, turn right after 5.8 miles onto Painted Cave Road. When the road gets down to one lane with a canopy of trees overhead, look carefully for the Painted Cave sign on the steep hillside by the rocks on the left. If you arrive at Painted Cave community, you've gone too far.
Season: Dry

Tip: You can go even at night!

Take a drive back in time. The Chumash have been in the area at least 10,000 years. The Chumash area covered San Luis Obispo to the north, down to Malibu, including this steep canyon overlooking Santa Barbara. They were mostly food gatherers, but also hunters. Another distinct group, the Island Chumash people, inhabited the Channel Islands.

Inside the cave are religious drawings and likenesses of coastal people fishing. This is art by the local Chumash Native Americans, created in the 1600s. These are not petroglyphs, or carvings in the rock, but pictographs, paintings on the rock. The paint pigments came from minerals, hematite, charcoal (black), red ochre (red) and diatomaceous earth (white). One picture is believed to be of a total eclipse of the sun.

Try to give yourself time to imagine it hundreds of years ago. Ideally, go here after checking out the Chumash exhibit at Museum of Natural History. The Painted Cave, at 2500' altitude, is less than 25 minutes from downtown. To get to Knapp's Castle from here, continue uphill to East Camino Cielo, and turn right one mile to the locked gate on the left.

Three-passenger Personal Water Craft; the best splurge in town!

Splurge!

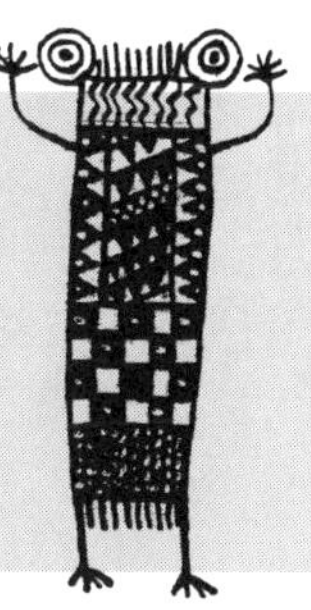

The whole life of man is but a point of time; let us enjoy it.
– Plutarch

You work hard all week; it's time for a break! Treat yourself and your little one. Create a lifetime memory. Go ahead, splurge. If it's a birthday party, a graduation present, or simply because you're worth it, sometimes the value is "priceless."

These are moments to share and relive in future years. Remember to take a camera or videocam for at least a minimal record of the event, but don't become a slave to the gizmo.

If you look closely at current pricing, you may find some way to fit it in your budget. Also, sometimes you can work things out with group pricing.

It's time to enjoy something special with your loved ones, and "don't look back."

Adrenalin junkies beware! Kart racing is habit-forming.

Go-Kart Racing

Rating: A+ for safety, education, dream-fulfilling
Ages: 6 and up
Directions: 101 South 35 minutes to Oxnard, exit Rice Rd., turn right, go 1.3 miles then turn left onto Sturgis, then right onto Discovery, then turn right onto Challenger, and go 300'. It's on the right at 1555 G Morse Avenue.
Contact: 654-1329 or www.jhrkartracing.com
Season: Call for schedule; most classes are on weekends

Tip: Half-day classes are the minimum you can sign up for

According to *Motor Trend Magazine*, Jim Hall Kart Racing School is one of the "49 cool things to do before you die." Children must be at least 6 years old to attend the half-day, 100-cc sprint carts classes of 18 which allow three half-mile, 11-turn track sessions of 10-12 laps. These karts are so low to the ground they are nearly impossible to flip. More than 32,000 students have learned racing and safe driving techniques from this school. It's so much fun, you'll probably be trying to figure out how to get your company to sponsor a team-building event here. Warning: The only downside of this activity is that you and or your children might become addicted to it!

A hot-air balloon ride approaches touchdown near Mission Santa Ines.

Flying High

Rating: A+ for unbelievable
Ages: 3 and up
Directions: Call first

- **Channel Islands Aviation:** For a picnic on one of the Channel Islands, this airline flies out of Camarillo or Santa Barbara for you. Let a Santa Rosa Island National Park Service Ranger give you a tour of the 53,000-acre island. You can customize your daytrip any way you want: fishing, hiking, bird-watching, tide-pooling or simply picnicking. You might see dolphins swimming as you fly 500' high across the channel!
  Contact: 987-1301 Ext. 0 or www.flycia.com

- **Red Baron Aviation:** This is a flight school that always has a teacher at the controls of the plane, and it takes up to three passengers for flights over Santa Barbara and Santa Ynez.
  Contact: 681-9200 or www.redbaronav.com

- **Spitfire Aviation:** Spitfire Aviation can take up to three passengers on scenic or photography flights over Santa Barbara and Santa Ynez.
  Contact: 967-4373 or www.flyspitfire.com

- **Unicorn Balloon Company:** Hot air balloon rides over Santa Ynez Valley include a champagne toast and flight video. Rides are available August through November, and February through April.
  Contact: 882-1214 or www.unicornballoon.com

- **Windhaven Glider Rides:** A car or truck tows only you and the pilot inside a glider plane, and you soar without an engine, over beautiful Santa Ynez Valley. Fantastic!
  Contact: 688-2517 or www.gliderrides.com

Three first-timers ride Segways downtown.

Segway Tours

Rating: A for unforgettable, futuristic, and adventurous
Ages: 14 years old minimum; under 18 must be accompanied by adult
Directions: 101 exit Garden St., toward ocean, right on Cabrillo Blvd., right after two blocks on Helena Ave. to 24½ E. Mason St.
Contact: For reservations, 963-7672 or www.segwayofsb.com
Season: 10-6 seven days a week. Any dry day; best when there's not too much traffic in town.

Tip: After you feel comfortable in training and ready to go out, train an extra 10 minutes for safety's sake!

Segway of Santa Barbara offers training and five different tours of Santa Barbara: Mission, Sunset, Old Santa Barbara, Butterfly Beach and Gaviota Coast Picnic. Most are guided tours. Tours are from 2 to 3.5 hours long and average about $25.00 to $40.00 per hour. The Gaviota Coast Picnic has you meeting them at El Capitan Canyon where you are trained, then you can explore the campground or cross under the freeway to explore El Capitan State Beach. It includes a catered picnic lunch in the glove box of your Segway.

The Old Santa Barbara Tour stops at the train station, Moreton Bay Fig Tree, De La Guerra Plaza, El Paseo, El Presidio, Santa Barbara County Courthouse, Kids' World, A.C. Postel Rose Garden, Santa Barbara Mission, Alice Keck Park Memorial Gardens and the Arlington Theatre. It covers six miles.

Powered by two lithium ion batteries, the Segway maximum speed is 12½ miles per hour. It is not classified as a motorized vehicle, but operates under the same rules and regulations as an electric wheelchair. It has access to places motorized vehicles usually can't go. It can go on sidewalks, through parks and El Paseo!

You can also rent a Segway by the hour, day or week.

Alisal Ranch: Besides horses, there's a petting barn.

Alisal Guest Ranch and Resort

Tip: Take the breakfast ride. Have a picnic at the lake.

Rating: A for peaceful, ranchy, pristine, variety, healthy
Ages: All
Directions: 101 North 4 miles, Highway 154 North 24 miles over San Marcos Pass, turn left on Highway 246, and in Solvang turn left on Alisal Road 2.6 miles. It takes about 50 minutes driving from Santa Barbara.
Contact: 688-6411 or www.alisal.com
Season: All year

Welcoming guests since 1946, here you have tennis, golf, horseback riding, fishing, kayaking, pedal boats, outboard boats, archery, ranch animal petting zoo, and a private lake on a 10,000-acre working cattle ranch adjacent to Los Padres National Forest. Simply put, it's world class. For children there is an arts-and-crafts program along with lessons in fishing, swimming and boating, and for seven-year-olds and up, lessons in horseback riding, golfing and tennis.

Air guns and canoes are also available. The staff works extremely well with children.

Riding in a Hummer on the dunes is an "E-ticket" ride.

Wild Rides

Rating: A for educational, outside and exciting
Ages: Use your judgment, but about 3 and up

Tip: Call for reservations and directions. Bring layered clothing.

Open-air vehicles offer fresh scents and different perspectives! Simply cruise State Street/Cabrillo Boulevard in a lime-green Shrek ride. Or get rowdy, four-wheeling the mountains, Pismo Beach or Oceano Dunes. It's all good!

Cloud Climber Jeep Tours

Whether you prefer paved East Camino Cielo with its gorgeous mountain-top views, back-country dirt trails, or Old Stage Coach Road and sunset tours, a Jeep ride is special. They can even pick you up at your house or hotel! Best in good weather at 646-3200 or www.ccjeeps.com

Pacific Adventure Tours

This company takes you on Hummer tours of Pismo Beach and Oceano sand dunes. Drive 75 minutes north to meet this non-stop roller-coaster. It's definitely an "E-ticket" ride! Seven days a week, 481-9330 or www.pacificadventuretours.com

Wheel Fun Rentals

Electric Cars, the polar opposite of others listed on this page. A real hit with little ones. Brightly-colored "Shrek" or "Scooby Doo" themed cars with no doors, for scooting around town. Also, mopeds and gas-powered mini-Hummers are available. This is a weather-dependent activity at 101 State St., and it's best to reserve first at 962-2585 or www.wheelfunrentals.com.

Channel Islands YMCA: loads of indoor activities.

Rainy? Dark? Cold?

"Wherever you go, no matter what the weather, always bring your own sunshine."

– Anthony J. D'Angelo

If you're faced with a rainy day or darkness at 5 p.m. and your children "Just wanna have fun" because they've been cooped up way too long, there's plenty to do!

Escape to Santa Barbara's outdoor classroom. Grab your galoshes, rain coats and hats and find the joys of puddle-jumping, leaf-boats and spotting the most earthworms. It's not bad weather, if you're dressed right . . .

After warm days, enjoy a nighttime safari in search of wildlife. Slowly drive a deserted road, and keep your high beams on in search of critters enjoying the warmth of the asphalt or dirt.

If it's a cold, clear night, check out www.familyeducation.com for night sky activities. Is it cold enough for a drive to the snow on East Camino Cielo?

If all these fail, it's time to climb the walls! All the following activities are indoors and most are open RIGHT NOW! Call to verify the operating hours. Go, Fun Hogs, Go! Please note that you don't actually have many rainy days here in The Sandbox, so keep some of these in mind for a good-weather day too! A mid-week family event can change your perspective, whether you're swimming indoors at the YMCA or painting ceramics.

Remember, "The only trips you regret are the ones you don't take."

A good workout at Santa Barbara Outfitters.

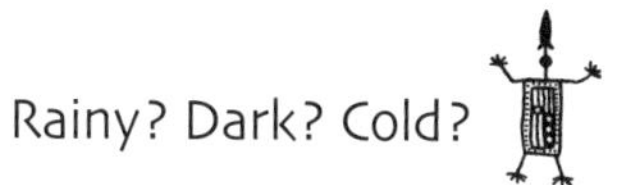

Climbing the Walls

Rating: A for exercise in any weather, almost any day

Santa Barbara Outfitters

Ages: Any ages as long as you sign a waiver for your child.
Directions: Garden Street exit off 101, turn away from the beach about a mile to Anapamu Street, turn left and it's at the corner of Anapamu and State.
Contact: 564-1007 or www.sboutfitters.com
Season: Store hours for children climbers, 10-6 Monday through Saturday, except Tuesday and Thursday when they can climb until 7 p.m. Sundays 11-6
Cost: About $3.00 to boulder without a belay, spotted by the parent. There are classes in which you can belay.

This is easily combined with a trip to the main public library across the street or 2000 Degrees ceramics painting adjacent at 1206 State Street.

UCSB Rock Wall (UCSB Adventure Climbing Center)

Ages: Adults must supervise children under 16
Directions: 101 North 7 miles, exit Highway 217 to the end. At the roundabout go right, then at the third signal turn left, and left again into the parking lot and pay for a parking permit at one of the automated machines in the lot. The Rec Cen II is across the street you turned from to enter the parking lot.
Contact: 893 3737 OR www.recreation.ucsb.edu.
Season: Private parties can be scheduled year-round; day passes for children of non-students/non-members can be purchased during summer only. Use of all sports facilities, including the pool, is included with student and community membership or with a day pass. 11:30 a.m.-10:30 p.m. Sunday through Thursday during the academic year. 11:30 a.m.-9:30 p.m. Friday and Saturday. It closes half an hour earlier than the Rec Cen.
Cost: About $8.00 for a day pass

Opened in 2005, this facility offers good prices, rental equipment and instruction. Up to 20 can climb the 30' imprint wall simultaneously – the largest climbing wall of its kind. After you pay to enter, you have access to all the other Rec Cen features such as the pool and ball courts. You must sign up at check-in when you arrive, and someone must belay you.

In summer, it's the beach; in winter, you need an indoor pool.

Indoor Pool Swim!

In the doldrums of winter, don't let weather or cold water deter you from swim lessons or a swim. All these offer lessons and possible drop-in swims. All you need is your towel and swimsuit and cash. Swim goggles make it more fun for little ones. Off-season swimming or swim lessons make the learning curve not-so-steep when summer comes around again.

- Anacapa Dive Center, 963-8917
  101, exit Garden, turn towards ocean, right onto Yanonali, left on Anacapa to 22 Anacapa Street
  Child-friendly, call for drop-in possibility and hours

- Santa Barbara Aquatics, 967-4456
  101 North 10 minutes, exit Fairview. Straight at signal over freeway towards ocean. Left onto Hollister to 5822 Hollister Ave. Call for drop-in possibility and hours.

- Wendy Fereday Swim School, 964-7818
  Call for drop-in possibility, directions, and hours.

- Channel Islands YMCA, 687-7727
  101 North, exit La Cumbre; right onto Calle Real; left at first signal, which is Hitchcock – 36 Hitchcock Way. Channel Islands YMCA (Santa Barbara YMCA) has a "family pass" available which enables your family to enjoy the pool as well as everything else in the facility. Taking advantage of one of these on a Tuesday or Wednesday after work and school really breaks up your week!

One-hour attention span is common while painting ceramics.

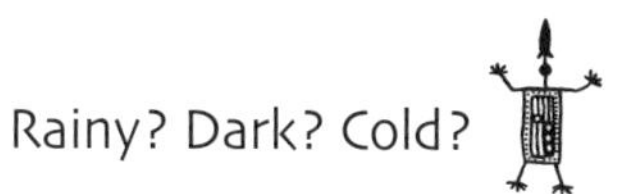

Ceramics Painting

Rating: A for creative, educational, and long conversation opportunities

Ages: Kids of all ages that like to paint; everyone can do it!

> **Tip:** 2000 Degrees is easily combined with Art Museum or Library across the street, or Santa Barbara Outfitters Indoor Climbing Wall next door! Color Me Mine offers unlimited colors, and often has discount specials for a day.

Grab a fired-once-already ceramic cup/plate/Christmas tree ornament/ sculpture, pick four paint colors (or more) and a brush (or sponge), and you're off on an artistic adventure! You can bring babies here to do tiny handprints and footprints that you, grandma and grandpa will love! This is a very healthy environment. If cost is a factor, call for prices or simply watch your child do one piece. It's best if you do a piece too, and you can share ideas/colors/chats. Pieces will be fired and ready in about four days, and they typically can ship to you if you won't be available four days later to pick it up.

Color Me Mine

Directions: Take 101 North 11 miles, exit Storke Road, turn left at the signal. Go through the signal at Hollister and turn into the Calle Real Shopping Center and it's at 7044 Market Place Drive, on the right towards Costco.

Contact: 571-1601 or www.goleta.colormemine.com

Season: 11:30-8 Monday through Friday, 10-9 Saturday and Noon-6 Sunday, approximately. Call for exact hours depending on the season.

2000 Degrees

Directions: Exit 101 at Garden Street, turn toward mountains about a mile, turn left on Anapamu Street and it's at the corner of that and State Street, at 1206 State Street.

Contact: 882-1817

Season: 11:30-8 Monday through Friday, 10-9 Saturday and Noon-6 Sunday, approximately. Call for exact hours depending on the season.

Buried in fun at My Gym.

Gym for Tikes

Tip: Call for fees, whether parent needs to attend, and if you can drop in.

My Gym

Rating: A for age span and variety
Ages: Three months to 12 years
Directions: Take 101 North, exit Hope Avenue, go straight at the signal onto Hope Avenue, turn left onto State Street to 3888 on the right. Parking is behind the building.
Contact: 563-7336 or www.my-gym.com
Season: Call for schedule and birthday party information

If you are enrolled in a class, you may attend a free play once a week. This is a parent or guardian-supervised activity. My Gym throws great birthday parties for youngsters.

A Kid's Gym at Channel Islands YMCA

Rating: B for can be convenient for adult workouts
Ages: Under 5, supervised by parent. 5-12, instructor-led, no parent required. 9-teenagers no parent required and no instructors.
Directions: Take 101 North, exit Hope Avenue, right at the signal, left into 36 Hitchcock.
Contact: 687-7727 or www.ciymca.org
Season: Monday through Friday, 4-8, Saturday 9-11 and closed Sunday. If you're not a YMCA member it's $10.00 per person per day, and they also have monthly rates. It's $25.00 for a non-member family per day.

The Rec Cen II has climbing walls and equipment rentals.

UCSB Recreation Center (Rec Cen)

Rating: A+ for variety, inexpensive, healthy
Ages: An adult must supervise children under the age of 16 at all times.
Directions: 101 North 7 miles, exit Highway 217 to the end. At the roundabout go right, then at the third signal turn left, and left again into the parking lot and pay for a parking permit at one of the automated machines in the lot. The Rec Cen II is across the street you turned from to enter the parking lot.
Contact: 893-3738 to clarify children policy or visit www.recreation.ucsb.edu to download waivers.
Season: Open to children of non-students/non-members during summer only. Children of students and members can come in during the school year for limited hours on the weekend between 10 a.m.-6 p.m.

Tip: Adults can buy a Day Pass or purchase a membership at 893-3738. Adults must bring a picture I.D. Bringing a child as a guest incurs a nominal fee.

This place is beautiful. It's like you're at a resort. The UCSB Recreation Center opened in 1995 and the adjacent Rec Cen II with rock wall opened in 2005. Work out in the gym, swim in the pool, play basketball, racquetball, volleyball or indoor hockey, and climb the 30' imprint rock wall – the largest climbing wall of its kind. There are additional fees for equipment and instruction. This place takes the "work" out of a workout.

If you like this place, locals can get an annual membership for greater access during the year for yourself or your child. What a healthy environment! So many sports, so little time! Such a deal!

Santa Barbara Library's five-level fountain.

Santa Barbara Public Library

Rating: A for educational, fun, follow child's passion
Ages: Readers or listeners, use your discretion
Directions: Exit 101 at Garden Street, turn towards the mountains about a mile, turn left on Anapamu Street, and it's at 40 E. Anapamu Street.
Contact: 962-7653 or www.sbplibrary.org
Season: Closed holidays, call for exact hours

Tip: Bring your library card! Check out unlimited children's videos and CDs downstairs

You know you're in for a good time when you first see the five-level fountain outside the front door. The fabulous door has university symbols, and after you enter, to your right is Faulkner Gallery with always-changing art exhibits. There is a large fascinating tropical fish tank in the children's section. Downstairs, there are CDs of music and videos for children.

But we've saved the best for last! Wonderful books, boatloads of them, lie inside. Let your imagination go wild or ask your child what they would most like to see, read or listen to a story about. Leprechauns? Fire trucks? Unicorns? Lighthouses? Horses? Santa Barbara Public Library has got you covered. There is no limit to the number of books you can check out. If the weather is fine you can also read on the roof! After, you can wander through adjacent La Arcada, and check out statues, shops and turtles outside Stateside Restaurant. Easily combined with Santa Barbara Outfitters Indoor Climbing Wall across Anapamu, Museum of Art next door, or 2000 Degrees ceramic painting at 1206 State Street. There is storytelling Tuesdays and Thursdays at 10:30 a.m.

Learn and be creative at the Museum of Art.

Santa Barbara Museum of Art

Rating: A for art lovers, cooperative children and education
Ages: Depends on the exhibit, the child, and any youth activities
Directions: 101 North, exit Carrillo, head inland to State Street and turn left to 1130 State.
Contact: 963-4364
Season: Any. Good for a rainy day. Tuesday-Saturday 11-5. Thursday 11-9. Sunday 12-5. First Sunday of the month free.

Tip: ArtVentures is dedicated to hands-on art education for children. The second Saturday of the month for ages 6 and up, 11 a.m. to 1 p.m. Call to reserve at 962-1661.

Easily combined with a visit to the neighboring Public Library, County Courthouse, 2000 Degrees or restaurants – all within a block. The gift shop is a great place to introduce young people to art. There is a children's art center next to the café.

Contact the museum for super high-quality art camps for youth during the summer. You've got to reserve early. The instructors and the facility are world-class.

Walking through the galleries to view art takes your child to another realm – creativity for self-expression and aesthetics. You can't put a price tag on creativity, but you can certainly get started right away if you're inspired via the art center and you can do rubbings on the front wall of the museum.

Check out the only intact mural in the United States by famous Mexican artist David Alfaro Sisqueiros, near the front steps of the museum.

Channel Islands YMCA welcomes paying non-members.

YMCA (Channel Islands YMCA)

Rating: A for almost 365 days a year
Ages: Preschool to 102
Directions: 101 North five minutes, exit Hope, right at the signal, left onto Hitchcock to 36 Hitchcock Way.
Contact: 687-7727 or www.ciymca.org
Season: Monday-Friday 5:30 a.m.-10 p.m., Saturdays 6:30 a.m.-7 p.m. and Sundays 11 a.m.-6 p.m.

Tip: Foosball and table tennis are always a hit!

As a non-member, you can drop in and pay once to play and swim! It's $25.00 per family or $10.00 per person. Call for indoor swimming pool hours and other activities such as basketball, foosball and table tennis. Remember to bring swimsuits, towels, and a padlock.

If you are a member of any YMCA, you can use this YMCA or the YMCA in Montecito (and its pool) at 591 Santa Rosa Lane, 969-3288. More Americans learn to swim from the YMCA than anywhere else. There are summer camps and youth clubs to join. The YMCA provides child care while you work out, called A Kid's Gym (see earlier in this chapter under Gyms for Youth entry). The YMCA also gives parents a break several times a year with Parents Night Out, when they host a dinner and a movie and anyone can leave their children while they enjoy a night out. Stay in touch for events such as Zoo To You, where keepers bring in exotic animals for an educational experience.

The museum's exhibits change periodically; the anchor remains.

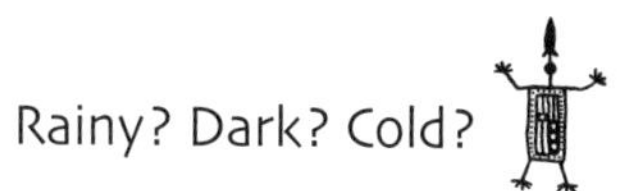

Santa Barbara Maritime Museum

Rating: B for educational, quiet, unusual, view
Ages: 5-95
Directions: 101 North 0.5 mile, exit Bath Street (Castillo), turn left at the signal (Haley St.), then left again at the next signal onto Castillo Street. Go 0.4 to the T intersection of Castillo and Cabrillo/Shoreline, and turn right onto Shoreline Drive. Take your first left into Santa Barbara Harbor parking lot. It's in the biggest white building, 113 Harbor Way.
Contact: 962-8404 or museum@sbmm.org
Season: Open Memorial Day to Labor Day except Wednesdays, 10 a.m.-6 p.m. Winter hours 10 a.m.-5 p.m. Closed Christmas, New Years Day, Thanksgiving and Fiesta Friday.The third Thursday of every month, it's free to the public.

Tip: There is a small children's area. Inspect the third floor Visitor Center, 884-1475.

Once you see the giant anchors, whale-hunting spear gun, and mini-submarine outside, you will know you have arrived at the Maritime Museum. It's next door to Endless Summer Bar-Café and downstairs from Chuck's Waterfront Grill. It was used as a Naval Training Facility from 1942-1995, and the Maritime Museum opened in 2000.

Exhibits vary and range from surfing to dive helmets. If the weather is foul, you'll at least *feel* like it's good, with exhibits like these. There is a nominal admission charge.

Need a date night? Children from 6 to 12 enjoy "Kids Night Out" the last Friday of every month. From 6 to 9 p.m., there are movies, food and activities.

High school and college students and older enjoy the "Shore to Sea" lecture series at 7 p.m. on the second Tuesday of the month. Some topics fascinate even younger students!

At Zodo's, it's not just bowling a ball!

Bowling

Tip: This is not your average bowling alley!

Rating: A for when it's rainy or dark, or you like bowling
Ages: Use your discretion; 5 to 9 years old and up is probably best
Directions: 101 North, exit Fairview, right at the signal at the foot of the ramp, right at the next signal onto Calle Real, and you'll see it on the right.
Contact: Zodo's Bowling & Beyond, 5925 Calle Real, Goleta 967-0128
Season: Sunday through Wednesday, 8:30 a.m.-2 a.m. and Thursday through Saturday 8:30 a.m. to 3 a.m.

Created by Paul Orfalea, founder of Kinko's Copies and a local Montecito resident, this may be the future for all the ailing bowling alleys nationwide. Orfalea believes youth need a place to go, and bowling alleys – tweaked with remodels, lights, music, and other visuals – can provide the destination. Loads of video games, plus billiards, round out the attraction. Like the Kinko's on Hope Avenue, this is the showcase location for the genre. It was good enough for Orfalea to rent the entire place for his children's private Halloween Party! There is bumper bowling to keep the balls out of the gutters, and even ball shooters for disabled or tiny ones so you only have to push it lightly to start the ball rolling toward the pins! Four nights a week there is bowling in the dark, and the rental shoes glow in the dark, lit up by black lights!

Mixing and matching craft pieces is fun!

Arts & Crafts Options

Art From Scrap

Rating: A for the conservation lessons as well as creativity you can teach
Ages: Use your discretion to see if it's right for your child
Directions: Exit Garden St., turn inland to Cota St.; it's on the corner at 302 E. Cota St.
Contact: 884-0459 for Saturday morning workshop info and store hours

If you or your child like to create, start with the recycled goodies at this place! Saturday morning workshops can give you a good start.

Arts Alive!

Rating: A+ for the staggering number of art, dance and other creative programs
Ages: Depends on which class you are interested in; you can start young!
Directions: Garden Street exit off 101, turn toward the beach, left on Cabrillo Boulevard, left on Calle Cesar Chavez to 1 N. Calle Cesar Chavez on the left.
Contact: 963-2278 or www.artsalivesb.com

Programs in ceramics, sculpture, painting, drawing, fabrics, costume design, sewing. In addition, there are classes in drumming, dance, music, songwriting and theatre arts.

Craft Essentials

Rating: A since kids of all ages enjoy being creative
Ages: 7 and up for classes
Directions: Take 101 North 7 miles, exit Turnpike; left at signal to Hollister and the shopping center at 187 Turnpike Road.
Contact: 681-3115

Do what you like, such as classes in beading, knitting, and crocheting; it's a great source for materials for do-it-yourself crafts.

Michaels

Rating: A for the diversity of things you can do with their materials
Ages: 5-12
Directions: 101 North, exit Fairview Avenue, at the signal turn toward the mountains, left into Fairview Shopping Center at 183 N. Fairview Avenue.
Contact: 967-7119 or www.michaels.com

Michaels "Kids Club" crafts workshops, Saturdays from 10-Noon, for children aged 5-12. Younger than 5 are allowed with an adult.

Whiz Kidz offers educational computer-related opportunities.

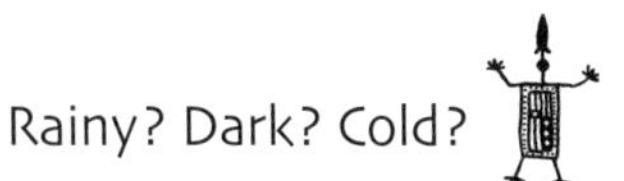

Whiz Kidz

Rating: A for opportunities to learn new software and improve in school subjects with the use of educational games
Ages: All
Directions: 101 North six miles, exit Turnpike Road, left at the signal to the shopping center at the corner of Hollister, 189 Turnpike Road
Contact: 696-9449 or www.whizkidz.net
Season: Generally after school hours in winter, closed Saturdays for private parties, and longer hours during summer

Tip: Drop-ins are welcome but more expensive.

Mainly a locals' destination, where you pay a day-use fee, or get a block of time, or purchase an annual membership fee, but it can be helpful on days that are rainy, dark or cold.

Whiz Kids offers a "homework club," tutoring, and computer workshops on filmmaking, programming and animation.

There are educational computer games for the age and subject matter of your choice. There is a color printer to complete homework assignments and there are even adult classes offered.

Use your discretion with this activity as computer games can be addictive. If your child has not played video games yet, do not bring them here! The educational section is too "close" to the gaming section.

East Beach Grill breakfasts, 1118 E. Cabrillo Blvd., 965-8805.

Chow Fun

"If more of us valued food and cheer above hoarded gold, it would be a merrier world." ***– J.R.R. Tolkein***

An elephant at the airport? Pizza in a lighthouse? Pancakes with a face? What's going on here, fun food? That's right . . . that's what this chapter is all about.

You know the routine with little ones, alighting for only 20 minutes at a restaurant; stay longer and face children under the table or climbing the booths.

There's an alternative. These dining destinations are designed to make it easy on you and your child. Why not go somewhere that they will enjoy; it makes life better for everyone.

There is a fun/food destination within a few minutes walk or drive, wherever you are in the Santa Barbara area.

Bon Appetit!

The jet and airplane view at Elephant Bar Restaurant.

 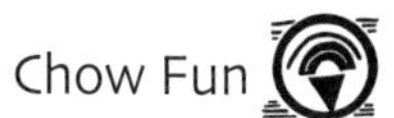

Elephant Bar & Restaurant

Rating: A for jets, fresh air, sunshine, and a children's menu
Ages: All
Directions: 101 North 10 minutes, exit Fairview Avenue staying straight, going over the freeway towards the ocean, turn right at the signal at the bottom of the overpass onto Hollister Avenue. After 1/4 mile, turn left at Griggs Place to 521 Firestone.
Contact: 884-9218

Tip: Best to sit at an outside table, the higher the better. Daylight hours.

Jets can be a stone's throw away. This is where the private jets land and park, and the scene can be fascinating. Every one of the seven items on the children's menu (for 10 years old and younger) includes a drink and dessert. Crayons and coloring materials are provided. This can be combined with a visit to the airport lookout parking lot at the southeast end of the runway.

Food for adults ranges from hamburgers to steaks, seafood and chicken; look for coupons that offer regular specials, often running in local newspapers.

Children love to eat pizza in a lighthouse . . .

 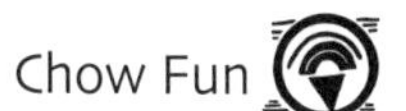

Pizza in a Lighthouse? Rusty's Pizza

Rating: A for location, fun, nautical interior, tasty
Ages: 3 up
Directions: 101, exit Garden, turn toward the ocean. Turn right at T intersection onto Cabrillo Boulevard to 15 East Cabrillo, about 3 blocks ahead, on the right before the lighthouse, turn right and then left into the Rusty's parking lot.
Phone: 564-1111 for delivery
Hours: 11 a.m. to midnight

Tip: You can enjoy a healthy meal here. The salad bar is fairly extensive and is a good value

Rusty's Pizza is Santa Barbara's most successful pizza establishment. Complete with a "boatload" of nautical items inside, Rusty's can capture any child's attention. Not that you need it, but there are video games too, like many other pizza parlors. There are Rusty's locations all over town, but this one is the most fun for the entire family. Rusty's also delivers to home addresses, hotel rooms – and even Alice Keck Park Memorial Garden!

Aren't pancakes one of children's basic food groups?

Pancakes (Everywhere)

Rating: A for kids menu, simple, decent food
Ages: All
Season: All year

> **Tip:** There's also decent food for adults!

- **Sambo's Restaurant** in the beach area, 216 W. Cabrillo (the original Sambo's restaurant became a chain and went nationwide in the 1970s until political correctness shut down all but this one, the first.) 965-3269
- **IHOP Downtown:** 101 North, exit Carrillo towards mountains, turn left onto State to 1701 State Street, 898-1886
- **IHOP Carpinteria**, 101 South exit Casitas Pass and turn right at the stop, then take the third driveway on your left, 566-4926
- **IHOP Goleta**, 101 North, exit Turnpike, right on Turnpike, turn right to 4765 Calle Real, 967-3030

Both companies offer a large kids' menu with crayons and coloring and games on the back.

Sambo's is open 7 a.m.-2:30 p.m., 364 days a year, and you have the waterfront/harbor directly across the street. All IHOP hours are approximately 6 a.m.-10 p.m. Sunday through Friday, 6 a.m-11 p.m. and Saturday 6 a.m.-Midnight. Of course you can find pancakes in just about any coffee shop, but these restaurants have made their reputations on pancakes.

Sand, toys, trains, and food all in one place!

Beach Grill at Padaro

Rating: A for outside, child-friendly, and unique
Ages: Toddler to adult
Directions: 101 South to Santa Claus Lane exit, and on the beach side of the freeway is the restaurant/playground
Phone: 566-3900
Season: Monday through Friday 11-8, Saturday 10-8 and Sunday 10-8 approximately. It's best to verify hours before going.

Hot Tips: You can bring in a dog if it's gentle and you are discreet. Listen for trains; it's like they're coming through the restaurant! A great place for a meal after a morning or day at Santa Claus Lane beach.

A large, grassy area, sand, playground equipment and sand toys. Sometimes it's open as early as 10 a.m. for light breakfasts. It's about the only restaurant a parent can eat at without worrying about their children bothering other diners. It's a good call when the weather is fine, but always bring extra clothing because the ocean breezes keep it cooler than other areas, and your children will want to stay a long time! If you would like to go to the beach, drive north 0.5-mile to the dirt parking lot at the portable toilet; there is a break in the boulders so you can walk on sand to the beach, and the railroad tracks are straight for better visibility. The railroad tracks at the restaurant are on a pretty sharp curve and it's amazing how fast some passenger trains come through there. Be sure your child's hand is in yours while you cross the railroad tracks.

Best table in the house: Shoreline Grill.

Shoreline Grill/Beach Café (Leadbetter Beach)

Rating: A for "almost in the water" view, sandy toes
Ages: All
Directions: 101 North, exit Castillo/Bath, turn left at Haley, then left on Castillo under the freeway to the end of Castillo at Cabrillo. Turn right onto Shoreline Drive. At the second signal, turn left into the parking lot and park. The restaurant is on the sand, 801 Shoreline Drive.
Phone: 568-0064
Season: The warmer the better, unless you just love the beach anytime.

Tip: Remember it's always cooler at the beach; call to confirm hours.

Where else can you dine with your toes in the white sand? Tables on the patio and on the sand. Leadbetter Beach here is the warmest in Santa Barbara since the cliffs block the prevailing northwest winds. Featuring outside showers, restrooms, grassy areas and a gentle surf spot, this is a popular beach. However, if you need solitude at low tide, you can walk around the point tidepooling and beachcombing to the "1,000 Steps" where you can walk up the stairs and back along the sidewalk and Shoreline Park.

Minnow Café is 50 steps from the commercial fishing dock.

Minnow Café (Harbor/Breakwater)

Rating: A for quick, decent, reasonably priced, outside
Ages: 3 and up
Directions: 101 North 0.5 mile, exit Bath Street (Castillo), turn left at the signal (Haley St.), then left again at the next signal onto Castillo Street. Go 0.4 to the T intersection of Castillo and Cabrillo/Shoreline, and turn right onto Shoreline Drive. Take your first left into Santa Barbara Harbor parking lot. Walk to 117 Harbor Way
Phone: 962-6315
Season: Open 6 a.m. to 4 p.m. 365 days a year. No-rain days are best.

Tip: Don't park on the other side of the fence from the boatyard where they spray-paint boats!

Location, location, location. Established in 1989, this tiny hole-in-the-wall serves good food to locals and tourists alike. It's located at the breakwater in the alley leading to the commercial fishing dock. It's 100 steps to the beach or Lil' Toot water taxi, or 50 steps to Paddle Sports where you can rent a kayak.

Cheeseburgers, puppy dogs, plain old grilled cheese, peanut butter and jelly sandwiches and corn dogs for little ones, as well as six salads, regular breakfasts, four breakfast burritos, six burgers, wine, beer, and more are served outside at picnic tables in the alley after you place your order inside. For the classic locals' sit-down lunch or dinner with the stunning harbor view, go upstairs to Brophy Brothers Restaurant (no reservations), but be prepared to wait your turn.

Longboards Grill: Free peanuts and treasure-chest toy!

Longboard's Beach Bar & Grill

Rating: A for the view, peanuts, toys, and videos
Ages: 1-101
Directions: 101 to Garden Street, turn toward the beach, turn right at the light at Cabrillo Boulevard, and turn left at the next light onto Stearns Wharf to 210 Stearns Wharf on your right, upstairs above The Harbor Restaurant (which is great for fine dining.)
Phone: 963-3311, same as Harbor Restaurant upstairs
Season: The warmer, the better if you're sitting on the outside patio, but there are plenty inside tables. A lot of tables have harbor/ocean views. Open 11:30-11 Sunday through Thursday, 8 a.m.-Midnight Friday and Saturday

Tip: Any child eating here gets his/her choice of a toy from the treasure chest. Help yourself to the peanuts in the big barrel; it's a great pre-dinner snack/activity.

Check out the old surfboards as well as surf videos on the big screen TV. If you're lucky, Santa Barbara's surf spot gem, Sandspit, will be breaking and surfers will be riding off the end of the breakwater. You'll love the elevator "views." Also children like to take a look in the fish tank downstairs near the rest rooms. Take a stroll around the wharf before you get back in your car to leave. There is valet parking.

If you bring your time-stamped parking lot permit to the restaurant, they will validate it with a sticker, and parking fees will be reduced when you leave! There is a patio for al fresco dining on the warmest or busiest days. Clear and sunny days make the harbor sparkle.

Note: If there's anyone in the family with an allergy to peanuts, choose another place to dine.

Do not overlook the Overlook Café!

Overlook Café (Santa Barbara Airport)

Rating: A if window table/outside table on a warm day!
Ages: All
Directions: 101 North 10 minutes, exit Highway 217, then exit at Sandspit Road. Turn right at the stop and it's half a mile down on your left at the elbow in the road.
Contact: 964-7793
Season: 6 a.m. to 7 p.m., no reservations accepted.

Tip: In order to get the outside or window table you want, put your name in and tell them you'll wait. Then walk downstairs outside in the back waiting area and check out the cool mechanical art, and walk around the airport.

There is no separate children's menu, but they do have children's items on the menu. It's kind of airport pricing, but there aren't too many views like this in town. You can watch jets land, take off, passengers embarking and disembarking, luggage being loaded and unloaded. Very cool for the right child. Can be combined with Under Your Nose chapter's lookout parking lot at the beginning of the runway, if you haven't had enough. Or head toward the beach and turn right into Goleta Beach Park for more fun.

A smoothie is delicious, healthy, refreshing and fun.

Smoothies! (Everywhere)

Rating: A for cool, delicious, fun, nutritional, close
Ages: Use your discretion
Directions: Call
Season: They open at 7 a.m. on weekdays and 8 a.m. on weekends. They close between 8 p.m. and 10 p.m., depending on the time change and location.

Tip: There's one within 10 minutes if you're anywhere between Montecito and Goleta.

How about a milkshake for breakfast, lunch or dinner? That's what this amounts to. A delicious and nutritional way to have a meal, and if you're in a hurry, you can take it with you and drink it in the car. If you've finished a hike or other fun, stop for a treat on the way home!

Blenders in the Grass

- 1046 Coast Village Road, #9, 969-0611 (Montecito)
- 720 State Street, 962-5715 (Downtown)
- 315 Meigs Road, 962-8881 (Mesa)
- 3973 State Street, 964-4465 (Uptown)
- 5743 Calle Real, 964-2788 (Goleta)
- 7014 Marketplace Drive, 968-7319 (Storke & Hollister)
- 6560 Pardall Road, 685-1134 (Isla Vista)

Jamba Juice

- 742 State Street, 966-4445 (Downtown)

Ice cream is a universal thing . . .

I Scream for Ice Cream!

Rating: A for close, cool, all ages and delicious

Whether you need a $1.19 single scoop from Rite Aid Drug Stores, a cone from McConnell's (first opened in 1949), gelato, soft-serve, or the latest ice cream blended with fruit and/or candy, these locations are only five minutes away, no matter where you are on the South Coast. These are listed from south to north so you can easily find the one nearest to you. Call for hours.

Carpinteria

- Foster's Freeze, 5205 Carpinteria Avenue, soft-serve, 684-3602
- The Spot, 389 Linden Avenue, 4 flavors close to the sand, 684-6311
- Rainbow Ice Cream & Yogurt Parlor, 751 Linden Avenue, 684-3118
- Robitaille's Fine Candies, 900 Linden, 8 flavors, 684-9340

Montecito

- Here's the Scoop, 1187 Coast Village Road, #9, gelato, 969-7020
- Gelateria Gioia, 1150 Coast Village Road, gelato, 969-9808

Santa Barbara

- Rite Aid Drug Store, 35 S. Milpas Street, 965-0787
- Great Pacific Ice Cream Company, 219-A Stearns Wharf, 962-0108
- Cold Stone Creamery, 504 State Street, 882-9128
- Ben & Jerry's, 305 Paseo Nuevo, 884-1055
- Rite Aid Drug Store, 825 State Street, 966-2760
- Sweet Alley, 1103 State Street, frozen yogurt too, 899-8304
- Foster's Freeze, 1924 Cliff Drive, soft-serve, 966-1336
- Rite Aid Drug Store, 1976 Cliff Drive, on the Mesa, 564-6599
- McConnell's Ice Cream, 201 W. Mission Street, midtown, 569-2323
- Via Maestra 42, 3343 State Street, gelato, 569-6522

Goleta

- Cold Stone Creamery, 5718 Calle Real, 692-1598
- Carvel, 147 N. Fairview, 967-4579
- Rite Aid Drug Store, 199 N. Fairview, 964-9892
- McConnells Creamery, 7034 Market Place, 968-0780
- Rite Aid Drug Store, 7127 Hollister Avenue, 968-2954

California Pizza Kitchen: Children love it!

California Pizza Kitchen

Rating: A for great kids' menu/activities, service, and cleanliness
Ages: All
Directions: 101 North, exit Carillo Street, turn right at the light. Turn right at Chapala Street and it's on your left at De La Guerra Street entrance to Paseo Nuevo.
Phone: 962-4648 or www.cpk.com
Season: Year-round

Tip: Counter tables allow you to see the pizza preparation!

The children's menu meets the needs of even the pickiest of eaters. The activity book is so cool that it keeps little ones entertained for at least as long as it takes for the meal to arrive, sometimes longer. It has really good food. Children enjoy the ice cream sundae that's $0.99 if you order a meal.

Ruby's Diner is like stepping into the 1950s.

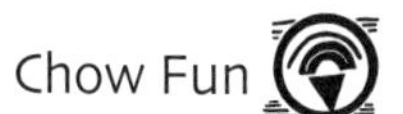

Ruby's Diner

Rating: A- for clean, history, excellent kids menu
Ages: All
Directions: 101 North one mile, exit Carrillo, right at the signal, right onto Chapala and it's in Paseo Nuevo Shopping Center at the intersection of West De la Guerra Street. You can turn into the underground parking structure on your left.
Contact: 564-1941 or www.rubys.com
Season: Open for breakfast, lunch and dinner

Tip: Order the Orange 50/50 milkshake!!!

Here's your '50s diner with the right combination!

Red vinyl booths, music, décor and waitresses that remind you of the '50s or educate you about the way it was in the '50s.

There are locations in eight states, and the extensive menu includes healthy options such as salads, turkey corn dogs and turkey hamburgers.

The '50s diner of today offers the Jitterbug Club for senior citizens, giving them discounts and special opportunities. Seniors can even save money on their family or grandchildren who they bring as guests!

Another current twist on the '50s diner includes eVites so you can go to the Web site, and customize online greeting cards to invite others to enjoy a meal with you!

It's just a fun place to go, and downright tasty food.

Around Santa Barbara, there's a trailhead only 10 minutes from you!

Trail Mix

Everybody needs beauty as well as bread, places to play in and pray in, where nature may heal and give strength to body and soul.
– John Muir

Leave no child inside! It's time to get out, and get acquainted! Today's child faces increasing threats to the environment, but her intimate relationship, her direct contact with nature, is decreasing. With the child in nature becoming an endangered species, here are recipes to encourage her to discover the hidden universe. The first step, a sense of wonder about nature, could lead toward an increased sense of wonder about the spiritual world.

With the National Wildlife Federation recommending "Green Hour" to parents, which encourages their children to daily enjoy nature outdoors, here are some tools to get that accomplished. www.greenhour.org

Let your child leave virtual reality behind for a bit, and respect herself for doing so, and at least achieve a balance.

Show her how to volunteer, experience nature or teach her how to take her camera for a walk. www.americanhiking.org

These trails vary from an easy five-to-ten minute walk to miles of fun. It's often easier for the short people when they have friends along so that it's more playful. You can make it more enjoyable with frequent breaks for water, snacks, a game or a quick biology lesson on a plant, animal or rock. You can also present the activity positively, "Would you like to go on the magic trail???"

In addition to providing good exercise and "ensuring a nap" or early bed time, trails teach them to care about the environment.

Remember, it's not so much the destination as the journey. You may not ever reach the destination, but if you shared, laughed and learned, your time was well-spent. Take time out for fun; it's as important to notice the bug and the fern on the way, as it is to see the mountain-top!

Minimum age is 12 years old for the top pools of the Seven Falls Trail.

Inspiration Point Hike/Seven Falls Hike

Rating: A for maximum view in shortest hike, plus a water feature!

Ages: 4- to 5-year-old children are more capable if with friends!

Directions: 101 North 2 miles, exit Mission. Turn right, continue past the Mission onto Mission Canyon Road. Turn right onto Foothill Rd., then take the next left to rejoin Mission Canyon Rd. Go left at the fork onto Tunnel Road for 1.2 miles to the end of the double-yellow line, and go right at the fork. You may want to drop the children and a parent at the gate to shorten the hike. Be careful to park with your tires completely within the line or you will be towed! The hike starts at the end of the road by the large water tank and metal gate across the road.

Contact: None

Season: Don't go uphill in the heat of the day!

Tip: This hike is aptly named; taking in the view from the sandstone boulders at the view point is excellent. Bring binoculars and water.

The hikes start at the gate. The paved road goes one half-mile up so kids have sure footing. Go left at the Y where the guard rail is. There will be a bridge to cross. Turn right. Just past the bridge, at the Tunnel trail junction, continue straight on Jesusita Trail, which crosses Mission Creek. Climbing on up the trail, you reach the stunning view point. Five miles roundtrip with 800-foot climb!

If you are adventurous and hike up Mission Creek instead of across Mission Creek, you'll reach a sandstone gorge with seven distinct little waterfalls and several deep pools. Use caution when rock-hopping or climbing huge boulders.

In spring, more water flows down Mission Creek: peak viewing time at Seven Falls, as the small sign says near the top of Tunnel Road. Later in the year, the water stops flowing and the water warms up more for swimming. In September of the driest years, you need to rock-hop and climb 1.5 hours up the creek bed to find a pool to swim in; higher pools have more water. To avoid climbing steep rocks in the creek bed, you can take the high trail on the left side of the creek, paralleling the creek, until you see a pool you like.

In awe of friendship with a wild butterfly named "Butter."

Butterflies Are Free,
a.k.a. Coronado Butterfly Preserve

Rating: A for outdoors, educational, easy-to-find and a short walk
Ages: 3 to adult
Directions: 101 North, exit Glen Annie/Storke Road, turn towards the ocean. Turn right on Hollister Avenue, turn left after about a mile at Coronado (no signal light). The preserve is at the end of Coronado Drive.
Contact: 966-4520
Season: November through March

Tip: Bring binoculars. Bring swimsuits if the weather is fine and walk all the way down to the beach. There are no lifeguards. The grove is a great place to view butterflies, but the huge field beyond it beckons to the active walker.

Monarch butterflies from all over the West Coast arrive at the 9.3-acre Coronado Butterfly Preserve to enjoy the winter. Eucalyptus groves have branches hanging heavy with the critters. No strollers or bikes. No butterfly nets allowed! It can be muddy, so bring shoes you're not worried about! As a long-term follow-up activity, do a Google search on "butterfly and grow" and buy a kit to grow butterflies! Watch them hatch and fly away! Very educational; taking it to the next level.

The Hammond's Trail is a beginner's trail.

Hammonds Trail & Beach

Rating: B
Ages: 3-10
Directions: 101 South four miles, exit San Ysidro Road. At the stop, turn toward the ocean. The road dead-ends at the ocean. To your right you will see a trailhead to the old Hammonds Estate.
Contact: None
Season: Spring and summer are best; morning light is magic.

Tip: Travel light, but combine the 10-minute walk with a day at the beach or tidepooling on a minus tide. Dogs are allowed on leash.

This trail is sandwiched between multi-million-dollar homes and features bougainvillea flowers and a canopy of trees. There is a nice lawn for a picnic and view of the surfers, channel and islands. At very low tide, you can return to your car walking on the beach the whole way.

Named to the National Register of Historic Places in 1978, the Hammonds Estate history includes a Chumash burial site and a memorial to it on the lawn above the beach.

Today, Hammonds Reef remains a popular surf spot, as it has been surfed since the 1960s.

Enjoying Santa Barbara's best view.

La Cumbre Peak

Rating: A for good air, quiet, view, 3,985 feet high
Ages: Toddler to adult, older children can find rocks to climb
Directions: 101 North four miles, exit 154 North. Go 8 miles and turn right on East Camino Cielo. Go 8.5 miles to La Cumbre Peak. To make a loop drive and return to Santa Barbara via an alternate route, continue east on East Camino Cielo past La Cumbre Peak two miles and turn right down Gibraltar Road to Mountain Drive, Sheffield Resevoir and to Foothill Road, about 30 minutes from the top.
Contact: None whatsoever
Season: The clearer the skies, the better!

Tip: Bring binoculars, a picnic lunch, a daypack, water. This can be combined easily with Painted Cave and Knapp's Castle; if you start at 9 a.m. you could do all three by 1 p.m.

After you pass the antennas and radio towers, park near the pine trees and locked gate that says La Cumbre Peak, on the right side of the road. The locked gate is to prohibit vehicles, except for emergency vehicles; it's certainly acceptable to enter by foot. Walk around the gate; on the paved road, veer right at the fork in the road. About 50 yards from East Camino Cielo you'll see a bench with a view! Sit and relax, or explore! There are many trails through the manzanita bush that you can explore to find your own rock with a view. The trailhead at the bench will take you 50 yards to a large boulder to climb and take in the scenery, or you can hike almost a mile farther to Cathedral Peak if you're an adventuresome, experienced hiker.

Horseback riding is available for children only seven years old.

Horsing Around

Rating: A+
Ages: Usually about 7-8 years old and up
Directions: Call for directions
Contact: See below
Season: In summer try to avoid the heat of the day. It's prettiest in spring when everything is green. In the autumn it's not too hot and there is less chance of rain.

> **Tip:** Memorable! Bring long pants, closed-toed shoes. Call for reservations.

There are four places to ride. Circle Bar B takes you up a coastal canyon with ocean and island views. Rancho Oso is near the Santa Ynez River off Paradise Road, and is more family-oriented, with camping, small cabins, and covered wagons available for less than $100.00 a night. El Capitan Ranch is near Circle Bar B and similar, but a little more pricey. Los Padres Outfitters takes you on pristine beach and back-country trips for a day or multiple days.

- **Circle Bar B Guest Ranch** 968-3901 or www.circlebarb.com, for children that are at least seven years old. Take 101 North 22 miles and exit Refugio Road. Turn right and go up the canyon four miles to Circle Bar B stables.
- **Rancho Oso Riding Stables** 683-5110 or www.rancho-oso.com, for children that are at least eight years old. This is in the heart of Los Padres National Forest. Take 101 North five miles and exit Highway 154. Go 11 miles over San Marcos Pass and the bridge, turn right on Paradise Road. Go 5 miles and you will see the sign on your right.
- **El Capitan Ranch** 685-1147 or www.elcapranch.com has trail rides, wagon rides, horse drawn carriages and Chuck Wagon Dinners. 101 North 19 miles, exit El Capitan Beach Road, turn right into El Capitan Ranch.
- **Los Padres Outfitters** 331-5252 or www.lospadresoutfitters.com Graham Goodfield leads Santa Barbara back-country and beach horseback riding trips that can be customized to your taste and time available. It's like going back to the days of cowboys and campfires. Children must be at least 12 years old.

Trails are about exploring and discovering.

More Mesa

Rating: A for fresh air and ocean views.
Ages: Toddlers and up
Directions: 101 North 6 miles, exit Turnpike Road, turn left one mile and turn left onto Hollister Avenue. Turn right on Puente, which becomes Vieja Drive, and go a mile. Look for parking when you see Mockingbird Lane. Those parking on Mockingbird Lane may be towed so park on Vieja. Walk uphill on Mockingbird. Although there is a barricade on the left with private property warnings, use the gap for pedestrians and continue onto the mesa.

Tip: Be sure *not* to park on Mockingbird Lane.

This secret gem, a 300-acre mesa, includes a degraded wetland. There are good ocean views over at the cliffs. There are no signs, so you'll have to keep your bearings, or retrace your steps back to the car. The mesa isn't used much because it is out of the way, but if you want quiet, wide-open spaces, this is it. Those heading toward the nudist beach below the cliff also use the mesa.

Hiking may take a back seat to water play: Rattlesnake Trail.

Rattlesnake Canyon Trail

Rating: A for All-Star
Ages: 3 to adult; kids will love the water on this hike.
Directions: 101 North, exit Mission Street and turn toward mountains. Follow the signs past the Mission on your left. Turn right at the T intersection stop sign at Foothill Road. At the next stop sign by the fire station, turn left onto Mission Canyon. At the fork in the road, stay right on Mission Canyon. Make a sharp right turn on Las Canoas. Just before Skofield Park is a stone bridge – that is the trailhead.
Season: Anytime except when it's storming or post-storm when it's muddy and slippery!

Tip: Bring a picnic lunch and water.

Don't let the name scare you from an excellent experience! Yes, there may be rattlesnakes like any other wilderness hike, but that's why the adult leads. There is water at the trailhead as well as quite a ways up. This is a forested trail with lots of shade and a good canopy above your head. Occasional poison oak shouldn't deter you. Perfect for children; it's a canyon hike that is shady, storybook-like, and features waterfalls, pools, various mushrooms in early winter, and if you're quiet and curious, there are birds and newts. It's 1.75 miles to the connector to Tunnel Trail, but that's not the goal; take one or more of the short hikes. It's moderate in difficulty and a 1,000-foot elevation gain. Park past the stone bridge in Skofield Park, or near the stone bridge.

A small boy finds solitude on a large rock at the Botanic Garden.

Botanic Garden

Rating: A+ for fresh air, quietude, beauty and educational value
Ages: 2 to adult
Directions: 101 North to Mission exit, turn toward the mountains. Follow the signs to the Mission, then take Mission Canyon Road past the Mission to Foothill Road. Turn right. At the next stop sign, turn left and follow the signs to the Garden at 1212 Mission Canyon Road.
Contact: 682-4727 or www.sbbg.org
Season: Monday-Friday 9-5; Saturday-Sunday 9-6 March-October. The remainder of the year, Monday-Friday 9-4; Saturday-Sunday 9-5. There are free guided tours daily at 2 p.m. (also Thursday, Saturday and Sunday at 10:30 a.m.)

Tip: Go during the cool of the day, early or late.

More than five miles of trails over 65 acres are perfect for walking, running, and exploring. Remember to bring appropriate footwear, and maybe a hat and a picnic lunch. Take your time and see how long you last! Try letting your children lead and see how long you can keep up! This is a great place to let your little one burn off some energy! There are classes for children as young as two years old.

The air seems fresher and more invigorating toward the beginning or end of the day. There are redwood trees. Visit the gift shop for great mementos of your visit.

Carpinteria Seal Rookery has a docent to explain everything.

Carpinteria State Beach Trail & Bluffs

Rating: A
Ages: Toddler to adult
Directions: 101 South, exit at Linden Avenue and turn toward the beach, go 0.6 mile through town to the avenue's end at the beach. Park along Linden Avenue (free, but time is restricted) or in Carpinteria State Beach parking lot (one block south)
Contact: Carpinteria State Beach 566-4984 or parks.ca.gov
Season: Warmer the better. During December to May the beach is for seals only.

Tip: Take binoculars. If you have little ones, spring for the day-use parking fee and drive to the southernmost parking lot to park, then walk south, saving about a mile walk each way along the beach or through the state park. Stay off the seal beach from December through May. Seal births begin occurring about mid-January!

You can park free on Linden Avenue and walk along the beach or through the state park. When you run out of beach, go up on the bluffs.

This area got its name in 1769 when Spanish explorer Gaspar de Portolá saw Chumash people making their wooden tomol canoes. Carpinteria means carpentry shop in Spanish. They caulked their canoes with the tar on the beach, and today just south of the campground a surf spot is named "Tar Pits." Some of the coast highway in Santa Barbara County was paved with a substance mined in the past right here.

City Bluffs Park, on 52 acres just south of the state park, makes a nice picnic area. Along the bluffs past Chevron Oil Pier is a nice view point above Harbor Seal Preserve. About 60 seal pups are born annually, and cliff-top volunteers educate visitors, monitor rookery activity, and count seals and births.

Officially named Carpinteria Bluffs Nature Preserve, the seal viewing area can also be reached from 101 South, exit Bailard Avenue, turn right at the stop to the parking lot and trailhead.

The bike/pedestrian path is flat, making it easy.

Bike Goleta

Rating: A for easy, unknown, interesting, active and family-friendly
Ages: Solid training wheels skills and up
Directions: 101 North 10 minutes, exit Highway 217, exit Sandspit Road. Turn left at the stop and take your next right into Goleta Beach Park, then turn right again, and once you pass the lawn on the right, turn right and park as far from the beach as possible. The bike path is on the mountain side of the park. Pedal onto the path turning right or going east, and it will take you out the entrance of the park where you just drove in (best to walk bikes here), then turn right at the stop sign onto the bike trail and you're on your way. At a major fork, do not turn left.
Contact: Bike map 961-8919 or email elindemann@sbcag.org.
Season: Any dry day

Tip: Teach your child to always stay on their own side and pull OFF the trail to stop. Bring a picnic or snacks and water.

This is the Santa Barbara Waterfront ride, on steroids. What it lacks in sheer beauty, it makes up for in length, quietude and fewer people. It goes past a small golf course many don't even know exists, and through a couple of neighborhoods before becoming even more beautiful on a solo bike trail again. You can go all the way to Modoc or Hendry's Beach, so the older your child gets, the farther you can go. Easily spend two to eight hours. For free maps and information of bike routes, contact 963-7283/www.trafficsolutions.info or Santa Barbara Bicycle Coalition at 568-3046/www.sbbike.org.

Biking Goleta has more of a "country" and wilderness feel than biking Cabrillo Boulevard bike path. There are no rental bikes available at the Goleta Beach trailhead. This can be combined with the playground at Goleta Beach Park, pier fishing/walking, a meal at Beachside Bar-Café, or a beach day. Bring a lock to lock up the bikes when not riding.

Who needs the mall?

Romero Canyon Hike

Rating: B for water, some shade and forest
Ages: 3 or 4 and up.
Directions: 101 South, exit Sheffield Drive. At the foot of the offramp, turn towards the mountains. At the next stop, turn right on Jameson. One hundred yards later it curves left and turns into Sheffield Drive. At the stop sign at East Valley Road, turn left, then make an immediate right onto Romero Canyon Rd. Turn right at Bella Vista Dr. After .25 of a mile, the trail head starts at a red gate.
Contact: www.santabarbarahikes.com
Season: Don't go in the heat of the day!

Tip: The clearer the day, the better the views!

The lower half of Romero Canyon Trail is the best section. Watch out for mountain bikers. A fire road crosses a bridge, then crosses a creek about half a mile up. Little ones may want to consider this as their final destination. For older children, look for a trail on the left after the second crossing. You'll head up the canyon on this trail and, at the junction, turn right back onto the fire road, following it about 4.5 miles back to the gate. Total hike is 6 miles. The first part is shady and along a creek that almost always has water.

Knapp's Castle, launching pad for the imagination.

Knapp's Castle

Rating: A for awe-inspiring, history, outdoors, short hike

Ages: 3 to adult

Directions: 101 North to Highway 154. Go six minutes and turn right on East Camino Cielo. About one mile past Painted Cave Road on the right, is a dirt shoulder for parking and on the left the first locked metal gate. Sign on the gate warns: "Right to pass revocable by owner." Actually, the beginning of the path is a public forest trail known as the Snyder Trail. Just before reaching another gate marked "Private Property – Keep Out," the Snyder Trail veers left below the ruins, which stand out on the horizon. View the property from the public trail only.

Contact: none

Season: It's inland and more than 2,500' high, so bring a sweater/coat if you're going early or late during off-season.

Tip: Get a National Forest Adventure Pass for your vehicle if you plan to leave it unattended by the road: after exiting 101 at 154, turn right onto State, then take your second driveway to the right to Big 5 Sporting Goods.

A wonderful place with a 180-degree view from Gibraltar Dam to Lake Cachuma. It's a quarter-mile walk to see the ruins, with pungent smells of chaparral, and vibrantly colored wildflowers in Spring. You may see California buckwheat, blooming yucca, toyon, deerbrush, laurel, pitcher sage, or scrub oak.

About 100 years ago, a cook at the Arlington Hotel in town decided to make his ranch in the mountains above Santa Barbara. There was a spring with laurels around it so he called it Laurel Springs Ranch. Later, George Knapp purchased the area. He built the Knapp College of Nursing here. He also built a mansion for himself "to make the tract a private mountain lodge that, in natural beauty and grandeur, would have few to equal it on the American continent." Five years later, it was destroyed by a brushfire.

Still later, actress Jane Fonda and Tom Hayden owned the property for a time while they were married. It's a world away and only a 25-minute drive from downtown.

Parma Parak is undeveloped except for tables.

Parma Park

Rating: A+ natural, active, family, healthy
Ages: 4 and up
Directions: 101 North, exit Mission towards mountains. Follow it until you reach the end. Turn left onto Laguna. At the stop, turn right onto Los Olivos. When you come to a fork in the road, veer left and drive to the end. At the stop, turn right on Foothill (192). Follow 192 to Parma Park in front of you as the road turns sharply right.
Contact: None
Season: Any dry day without low clouds; the clearer, the better.

Tip: For those who like peace and quiet, views. No playground equipment here.

This is a huge park and it has some good hikes. Trails can be wide and there are a couple of picnic tables and nice views at the end. It's not terribly strenuous.

About 50 yards after you see the picnic tables at the beginning of the hike, there is a small trail that crosses the creek, if you prefer not to take the trail that is as wide as a car.

The wide trail is a good challenge, 45 minutes up to the hilltop viewpoint with picnic tables. About 50 paces past these tables, there is a fork at the "Caution" sign. Go left to a dead end. Go right to make it a loop trail and a longer way back home.

Dogs love this place for all the odors of plants and animals. Mountain bikers like this park, too. There are no creeks, other than at the beginning of the trail, and there is no shade.

Ennisbrook Trail is flat, shady and woodsy.

Ennisbrook Trail

Rating: A for creekside, flat
Ages: Must be able to stay on a trail. 3 to adult
Directions: 101 South, exit Sheffield Drive, turn left at exit, then right onto frontage road North Jameson. Stay left at the fork onto Sheffield Drive. Turn left after .25 miles onto San Leandro. Go 0.7 mile to the parking area near the white picket fence. The trailheads are on both sides of the creek.
Contact: None
Season: Any except rain

Tip: Watch for poison oak and don't bring a dog that will run in it.

Here's a flat, oak-canopied, creekside trail perfect for young hikers who can stay on the trail. You are hiking in the heart of Montecito on one of Montecito Association's trails. It follows San Ysidro Creek about one mile.

If you join Montecito Trails Foundation (568-0833) for $25, your membership includes a free map of more than 300 miles of trails.

It's a short Rancho Oso hike to the waterfall.

Rancho Oso Guest Ranch & Stables

Rating: A+ for cowboy-types and outdoors people who don't like to cook
Ages: 8 years old and up minimum for horseback rides
Directions: 101 North 4 miles, 154 North, exit Paradise Road after 10 miles, and it's about 20 minutes more to 3750 Paradise Road.
Contact: 683-5686 or www.rancho-oso.com
Season: Summers can get hot back there and has more flies. Spring and Fall are ideal, but any time it's dry will do.

Tip: Bring your swimsuit, hiking boots, bike, camera and tennis racquet! Reserve dinner in the lodge by 2 p.m.

This is for those who feel a one-hour horseback ride isn't the complete answer – they need more fun! Public accommodations on the 310 acres start at about $59.00/night. You sleep in insulation-free covered-wagon replicas around a camp fire pit, or minimalist bunkhouse cabins. Hot breakfast and dinner are available in the stone lodge, built in the early 1900s as a residence. No experience required for guided horseback rides on scenic trails surrounded by Los Padres National Forest. Enjoy hiking, biking, volleyball, tetherball, tennis, swimming, basketball, horseshoes, spa, playground, satellite TV, data port and a store. Horseback rides available (about $30.00 per hour) if you pay for overnight. A unique wilderness trail along a year-round spring-fed creek leads to a special place at the base of a 40' cascade. One mile round trip.

It's a tight squeeze on some of this trail!

The Playground

Tip: Bring water, food and stay on the trail.

Rating: A for rock hopping, views, and variety
Ages: 4 or 5 on up if you hold their hand atop rocks
Directions: 101 North 4 miles, exit Highway 154. Go 7.5 miles and turn left at West Camino Cielo/Kinevan Road. Go 2.4 miles and find a power line crossing the road. It's near the Tanbark Oak sign on the right side of the road. The trailhead is to the right of an oak tree, near the pole that is one foot from the left side of the road.
Contact: None
Season: Spring and fall are best, hike mornings in summer, and winter when it's dry.

It's an easy, sometimes shady slope downhill 30 minutes to an acre-sized rock outcrop that is very fun to scramble on and around. Be sure to watch out for poison oak along the trail. There are a couple of small caves and outstanding views of the Goleta Valley. Watch for rattlesnakes in the crevices. Bringing their friends or taking breaks keeps childrens' minds off the moderate difficulty. Children in backpacks aren't ideal since, in a couple places, you must bend over in order to duck branches, and their heads would scrape the brush.

Enjoy a picnic lunch from atop the rocks overlooking Santa Barbara Channel and then head home. Very experienced hikers can search east of the rocks for the Narrows, a 400-yard long crease in the sandstone, carved by water. It's not easily accessed but once you're inside (sometimes you need flashlights) it's worth it.

Cold Springs East Fork Trail has pools to cool off hot hikers.

Cold Springs East Fork Trail

Rating: A+ for the best hike; water, pools, shade, slippery slides
Ages: Six and up in the canyon; 10 and up to Montecito Peak
Directions: 101 South three miles, exit Olive Mill Road, turn left at the stop, and 0.5 mile after you pass the gas station, stay straight and it turns into Hot Springs Road. Continue straight to the top of Hot Springs Road to the T-intersection of East Mountian View Drive. Turn left, go 1 mile and the trailhead is immediately before Cold Springs Creek, adjacent to where Cold Springs Creek flows over the road.
Contact: None
Season: Any, except rainy days

This is the most bang-for-the-buck hike around Santa Barbara.

It's about .75 mile to the pools, 1.75 miles to the power line overlook, 3.5 miles to Montecito Peak, and 4.5 miles to East Camino Cielo Road. There are two trailheads not far apart right before the creek crosses over the road. The first one (Ridge) you come to is the fastest way to Montecito Peak and is not so shady. The second one (East Fork) goes up the canyon in the shade next to Cold Springs Creek for 0.25 mile, to the trailhead to Cold Springs West Fork (trail sign on the left), and a bench on the left nearby.

About 0.75 mile from Mountain Drive, the trail crosses a creek. You can turn and start rock-hopping up the creek, or wait until the trail re-crosses the creek another 10 minutes up and start looking for pools there. At 1.75 miles, you're at the power line towers up on the ridge, a great Santa Barbara view and first stop if you're up early and headed for Montecito Peak. After that, you'll reach a lone eucalyptus tree, which is a great place for your second stop. The trail is well marked, but you'll see a steep trail forking to your right about one mile up from the tree. Take that and in 10' you'll take a left at the Y. About 50 feet up, you'll see the summit! In about 0.25 mile you're at Montecito Peak. On clear days you can see UCSB to south of Rincon and all islands.

The round-trip 2.75-mile West Fork trail (for serious hikers) forks to the right after the Santa Barbara Land Trust sign, follows the creek bed rock-hopping, goes to the left of a smaller waterfall on your right, to 150' high Tangerine Falls on your right.

Wetsuits are a must for Santa Cruz Island snorkeling.

Get Outta Town!

Remember that happiness is a way of travel – not a destination.
– Roy M. Goodman

From ostriches in the Valley to hyenas in Moorpark, from 164-foot Nojoqui Falls to boating into 60-foot sea caves at Santa Cruz Island, from a light house at Port Hueneme to windmills in Solvang, sometimes ya just gotta go!

When you consider it takes 45 minutes to drive to work or school if you live in a big city, you can surely drive 45 minutes to show your child dog-size miniature horses, right?

Remember, if it's overcast and cool in Santa Barbara, it's often clear and warm over the hill, with the Santa Ynez Mountains blocking the marine layer.

If Santa Barbara seems like a sleepy little town, there's a huge market down in Ventura and Oxnard, 37 minutes away, that supports roller and ice skating rinks, water parks, childrens' museums and miniature golf.

Note that drive times may vary during rush hour or Sundays in the afternoon heading south on Highway 101, but these are closer than you think!

Port Hueneme Lighthouse is open one precious day a month!

Port Hueneme Lighthouse (Oxnard)

Rating: A for educational, historical (Lighthouses are the castles of America)
Ages: All ages
Directions: 101 South 35 minutes to Victoria Avenue exit. Turn right onto Victoria Avenue, go several miles to Channel Islands Boulevard. Take a left onto Channel Islands Boulevard and make a right on Ventura Road. Turn right onto Hueneme Road. Hueneme Road leads right into Port Entrance.
Contact: (310) 541-0334
Season: You must call for reservations; open one day per month: the third Saturday from 10 a.m. to 3 p.m.

Tip: Can be combined with the Gull Wings Children's Museum trip. You must arrive before 2:30 p.m., and a photo identification is required for everyone 18 years of age and older.

If you're into lighthouses, this is a must, considering the next public lighthouse is hours of driving north. North of Santa Barbara, Pt. Conception Lighthouse is on private land, and Pt. Arguello Lighthouse even farther north is on government property at Vandenburg Air Force Base.

Port Hueneme lighthouse is very modern looking. It's adjacent to the beach in an area you wouldn't normally pass. Even if it looks new, it still has a great history, and the lighthouses before it on the same property were important to coastal traffic.

This is a history lesson, really. It's about California's coast, offshore navigation, transportation and the military. If it weren't for the lonely lighthouse, everything else along the coast wouldn't be what it is today.

To make your trip even more worthwhile, you can combine it with downtown Oxnard's Gull Wings Children's Museum.

You can rock wall climb at Gull Wings Children's Museum.

Gull Wings Children's Museum (Oxnard)

Rating: B+
Ages: 2-11 can easily spend 45-60 minutes here
Directions: 101 South 45 minutes, exit Oxnard Boulevard which turns into Oxnard Boulevard. Go two miles to Fourth Street. Turn right and it's four blocks down on the left side at 418 W. Fourth Street
Contact: 483-3005
Season: Tuesday to Sunday 10 a.m.-5 p.m., $4.00 per person. Under 2, free.

Tip: If it's the third Saturday of the month, this activity can be combined with Port Hueneme Lighthouse free tour (see Port Hueneme Lighthouse).

This place provides interactive, educational fun for children and families. There is a real car to play in, grocery store to "shop" in, black light painting, a sabot dinghy to "sail," small touch tanks, a train and a space ship.

It's certainly not on the scale of the children's museums in Los Angeles, San Jose and San Diego, but it'll do just fine, thank you. The only other children's museum is in Santa Maria, 75 minutes north of Santa Barbara.

"Toddler time" is Tuesdays at 11 a.m. and after-school crafts is held weekdays at 3:30 p.m.

Shows illustrate how students train animals.

 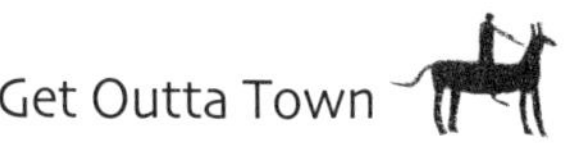

America's Teaching Zoo (Moorpark)

Rating: A for unique
Ages: Toddler up
Directions: 101 South 54 miles, exit Highway 23, which turns into 118 East. Go 8 miles, exit Collins Drive, turn left at the base of the offramp. Go about 0.5 mile when you see University Drive on your left, turn RIGHT into a parking lot, and immediately right and follow signs to 7075 Campus Road.
Contact: 378-1441
Season: Saturdays and Sundays 11 a.m. to 5 p.m. The demonstrations are at noon, 1 p.m., 2 p.m., and 3 p.m. The carnivore feeding is at 3:45 p.m.

Tip: Summer can get hot and have the biggest crowds. Bring a sack lunch to enjoy at the small picnic area.

Lions and hyenas and ostrich oh, my! On weekends, the Moorpark College Exotic Animal Training and Management program offers the public a five-acre zoo of 150 animals to explore, viewing exotic animals being fed, and interesting 15-minute demonstrations that focus on particular animals or groups of animals.

It's not Santa Barbara Zoo; it's a vocational program offering education in the care and training of animals and the presentation of educational shows utilizing animals. Monday through Friday, students receive instruction in modern techniques of zoo keeping including nutrition, restraint, and veterinary procedures. College students in the program receive classroom instruction in the techniques of presenting educational and entertaining animal shows. Then they refine their understanding of these principles and develop their own style by actually performing for you on weekends.

Here's an educational activity where students become teachers and you reap the benefit.

"Quads" (left) and inline skates are both fun.

Skating Plus (Ventura)

Rating: A for retro, party-place, any good weather, good music, any weather.
Ages: If your child wants to skate, they have the skate size
Directions: 101 South 32 miles, exit Victoria, left at the signal, left onto Victoria, 0.25 mile and left onto Walker St., right on Mesa Verde Ave. to 1720 Mesa Verde.
Contact: 656-2121 or www.skatingplus.com
Season: Call to verify hours before you go.

Tip: Good for a family atmosphere.

At least one parent with a child pining for roller skates has found this place to be more sensible to determine if there really is a passion and skill in skating that warrants the purchase of a pair of skates. Whenever you go here, your skates fit!

Whether it's old-school "quad" roller skates or in-line skates you choose, this facility fits the bill. It offers classes, a skate shop including hockey equipment, and even a "Junior Session" Saturday mornings for children up to 10 and their parents, when fun kids music is played. You may want to save money during Family Night or Cheap Skate Night. With the lights turned down and your child saying, "That's my favorite song!" it's a fun atmosphere.

Miniature golf is available every day of the year!

Golf N' Stuff (Ventura)

Tip: Check out their Web site for coupons.

Rating: A for open every day, variety, pure entertainment
Ages: 3 and up
Directions: 101 South 31 miles, exit Victoria. At the signal at the end of the ramp, turn left. Turn left at the next signal, which is Victoria and go under the freeway. At the second signal, turn left on Moon, which turns into Walker. 5555 Walker Street.
Contact: 644-7131 or www.golfnstuff.com
Season: Open 365 days a year, 10 a.m.-10 p.m.; longer on weekends/holidays.

It's not educational, and it's definitely not nature, but children love it. Smaller children like the miniature golf. Remember: in regard to the number of putts: "It's not how many, it's how fun." Also, the more putts you take, the more you get for your money!

You must walk through the arcade to get to the golf and rides. Smaller children can ride as go-kart passengers when an adult drives. For older children there is a laser tag arena, an arcade, and bumper cars. Bumper boats are best left for 12-year-olds and up as they are challenging for younger children to navigate.

This arch is 200 yards from Anacapa Island landing cove.

Channel Islands National Park

Rating: A for educational, conservation, boating, wildlife
Ages: Even three-year olds can camp the east end of Santa Cruz
Contact: For boat transportation, contact:
- Condor Cruises in Santa Barbara, 965-1985 or www.condorcruises.com
- Island Packers in Ventura, 642-1393 or wwwislandpackers.com

For general information, contact
- www.nps.gov
- Visitors Center in Ventura, 658-5730
- "Outdoors Santa Barbara" visitors center, located in the Santa Barbara Maritime Museum building at 113 Harbor Way is a Channel Island information center and has an excellent map, 884-1475 or www.outdoorsb.noaa.gov.

Season: September and October are the best months as they are the least windy.

Just offshore, in your own backyard, is a national park consisting of San Miguel, Santa Rosa, Santa Cruz, Anacapa and Santa Barbara islands. Most are less than 30 miles away. There's kayaking, beachcombing, fishing, hiking, snorkeling, diving, birding, surfing and sailing. And yet very few people visit, even for a day trip.

There are often dolphin shows off the bow or in the distance. Summer provides the warmest water and air, as well as a chance to see blue whales.

Beginners might start with a day-trip to Anacapa Island, only 11 miles from Channel Islands Harbor in Oxnard. It's the easiest trip, but steep cliffs reserve it for parents and children that are responsible.

Santa Cruz Island is the largest and has a beach and campground on the east end that is a more friendly place to snorkel, kayak, hike and camp. It's a longer trip, however one-day guided kayak trips are available out of Santa Barbara. It has the largest sea cave on the West Coast.

Santa Rosa Island is the second-largest, offers ranger-led tours, and is much farther away. It has fewer visitors and is for the adventurous and those with strong stomachs, or those who take the 45-minute flight to an air-strip, which is a ten-minute walk from the campground.

San Miguel has palm trees on a white sandy beach, a caliche forest, and its 2,000-4,000 breeding pinnepeds in season are staggering.

Santa Barbara Island is 38 miles from the mainland! Boat trips are well worth the effort when you snorkel among sea lions but camping is spartan! Visit this island last.

How fast can you do a lap at Slotcar Raceway?

Slotcar Raceway (Oxnard)

Rating: A for always worth the drive
Ages: Approximately 3.5 years and up
Directions: 101 South 37 miles, and immediately after the long bridge over Santa Clara River, exit Ventura Road straight into Wagon Wheel Plaza, at 830 Wagon Wheel Road in Oxnard. It's directly across the street from the offramp.
Contact: 988-8044
Season: Monday through Friday Noon to 8 pm. Saturday 10-10 and Sunday Noon to 6 pm. Closed Thanksgiving Day, Christmas Day and Fourth of July.

Tip: It's best to verify hours and directions before you go. Also, before you leave, ask for clear directions on how to get back to 101 North. Can be combined with Oxnard Children's Museum or Port Hueneme Lighthouse, or adjacent ice skating.

This is like electric trains on steroids! Only come here if you want to create childhood memories!

About as long as a pencil, slotcars have a piece of metal under the chassis that fits into one of eight slots around a 150' curvy track with five straight-aways. They also have wires that connect into the track for power that makes them go incredibly fast. Experienced drivers can complete a lap in 3.9 seconds.

Established in 1995, Slotcar Raceway charges per half-hour for a rental slot car, controller, and power. Your child will never forget it! It's world class.

Children that are only three or four years old can do it successfully because you can rent cars that have governors on them that keep them from going too fast and crashing at sharp turns.

Note: Can be addictive.

Ventura's water park appeals to many ages.

Ventura Aquatic Center Water Park

Rating: A for family, safety, hours of fun
Ages: All ages except teenagers who might be too "cool" for this
Directions: 101 South 35 minutes, exit Highway 126, exit Kimball Rd., turn right; the water park will be on your right at 901 S. Kimball Road, in Ventura Community Park before Telephone Road.
Contact: 654-7511 or www.cityofventura.net / www.venturacommunitypark.org
Season: Closed Easter Sunday, but open Spring Break, and all holidays including Labor Day Weekend.

Tip: This is a great value. Some children prefer goggles as the chlorine bothers their eyes.

Hurricane Harbor at Magic Mountain has warmer air and is bigger, but Ventura's water park doesn't take a full-day commitment! It's easily doable in three to four hours round-trip. The trouble with this adventure is getting everyone to leave, once you get there! Opened in October, 2005, a zero-depth entry allows even the smallest tykes to play. Maximum depth is 1.5' so the water playground is especially great for smaller children. Children at least 48" tall love the two 20-foot high water slides. The green slide is completely enclosed and almost pitch-black inside; it's probably the favorite. The blue slide is a half-pipe and you probably go faster! There is also a 25-meter recreation pool from 3' to 4.5' deep with temperatures varying from 82 to 84 degree year-round. Multiple-day family passes are available for a discount.

Water playground, or float down the continuous river; it's your choice!

Casitas Water Adventure (Ojai)

Rating: A for water and can be combined with bike rental or lake activities
Ages: Walking age up to young teenagers
Directions: 101 South, go 12 miles and exit Highway 150 in Carpinteria. Turn left at the stop and go 13.5 miles to Lake Casitas on your right. Park outside the entrance and save Day Use fees; walk 50 yards to the water park.
Contact: 649-2233 or www.lakecasitas.info
Season: From Memorial Day to mid-June it's open on weekends. From mid-June to mid-August, it's open seven days. From mid-August through Labor day it's open only on weekends.

Tip: Bring goggles to minimize chlorine stinging eyes!

Sure you can drive an hour and a half to Six Flags Hurricane Harbor in Valencia with all the teenagers, but here you have a perfect youngsters' water park, complete with a "Lazy River"!

The zero-depth pool goes to a deepest of 18". There are waterfalls, slides, stairs, and jet sprays. The bright colors add to the feeling of fun.

In 2006, the 1,200-foot slow-moving river was added. It carries visitors on park-provided inner-tubes, past waterfalls and jet sprays. There are plenty of lifeguards, and a limited number of free life jackets are available. Additionally, there are coin-operated hot showers, locker rentals, a snack bar and sundries available.

Grassy areas are ideal for picnics. This is a very family-oriented facility.

That alone is worth the trip, but you can combine it with a Cycles 4 Rent surrey ride or bike rental inside Lake Casitas Recreation Area; call 304-6544 for more information. There are also motor boats for rent, and even fishing by full moonlight four times a summer!

You can climb atop a train at Travel Town Museum!

Triple Train Heaven (Los Angeles)

Rating: A+
Ages: 3 and up
Directions: 101 South 83 miles, exit Highway 134 East 3.9 miles, exit Forest Lawn Drive, right onto Forest Lawn Drive, left onto Zoo Drive and it's right there, at 5202 Zoo Drive.
Contact: For Los Angeles Live Steamers, listen to a recorded message (323) 662-8030 or telephone (323) 661-8958, www.lals.org
Season: Any dry Sunday. Sundays are best because that is the only time the live steamers run. The museum and GP&S Railroad are open other days than Sunday.

Tip: Leave Santa Barbara at 9:30 a.m. and bring a picnic lunch and camera/video cam

Your self-guided Triple Train Heaven Tour begins with Los Angeles Live Steamers; it's where Walt Disney got his start in fun! Steam-powered trains, anyone at least 34" tall and not more than 350 lbs. can ride on top of for free, courtesy of this non-profit organization. It's only open 11 a.m.-3 p.m. Sundays, weather permitting except the day before Memorial Day, and the first Sunday in October.

Adjacent at 5200 Zoo Drive is Travel Town Museum, with huge train engines and interesting railroad cars as well as indoor exhibits and an outdoor miniature train you can sit inside. (323) 662-5874 or www.laparks.org/grifmet/tt/index.htm.

Finally, exit Travel Town Museum parking lot and turn right and go about 10 minutes (past the zoo) to GP&S Railroad at Los Feliz Boulevard and Riverside Drive. This train is even larger than the previous two! Closes at 5:30 p.m. (323) 664-6788 or www.gprah.com.

If you haven't had enough fun, children up to 100 lbs. can go on the adjacent Pony Ride. It's rare because it's not hand-led; each child is alone on a pony in this one-way course. It's priceless! This could be the best "Outta Town" day in the book!

"The best pizza in the world," says one youngster.

Chuck E. Cheese (Ventura)

Rating: A for alone in its "class"
Ages: Toddler to 12
Directions: 101 South 35 minutes, exit Telephone Road. Turn left at the light onto East Main Street then quickly get in the far right lane to turn right onto Telephone Road. You'll see Chuck E. Cheese immediately on your left. Take your next left into the parking lot and left again to park at 4714 Telephone Road.
Contact: 644-9777 or www.chuckecheese.com
Season: A place to go indoors on a rainy day and get active. Most enjoyable if you can avoid weekend crowds. Call to verify hours.

Tip: You can sometimes find coupons to print out at their Web site. Be sure to catch the show in the other room as soon as it starts as showtimes are sporadic.

This is one restaurant/game parlor you'll never forget. Children claim they serve the best pizza in the world. Every family should go at least once by the time the children are seven. It's Ventura's Disneyland. Dinner out has never been so wild. You have your hand and your child's stamped at the door so you can only leave together. You buy tokens to put in electric games and rides, sometimes receiving tickets back for winning. You can exchange these tickets for prizes before leaving. There are Chuck E. Cheese (he's a mouse character) shows on stage. Older children migrate to video games. It's the polar opposite of Channel Islands National Park. Children love it; adults, be prepared!

It's real steam, a real engine, and you ride on top!

Fillmore & Western Railway Company

Rating: A if you're under 8 or just love trains
Ages: You'll know if you're included!
Directions: 101 South 35 minutes to Ventura, and after you see the Seaward Exit, take the next exit to Highway 126 East about 20 minutes to Fillmore, and turn left at the signal at Central.
Contact: (800) 773-8724 or (805) 524-2546 or www.fwry.com
Season: Call for schedule or festival dates

Tip: Don't miss the annual festival!

Fillmore & Western Railway Company is cool any day of the year. Even better is the annual two-day spring festival in this small city. You see kids that are 75 years old, still enjoying trains. And why not? You can be an engineer on an 1891 Steam Engine, ride on the top of a miniature steam train, or take a vintage train ride complete with bank robbers and sheriff drama.

For real excitement, arrive at 9:45 a.m. on festival weekend in March, buy your vintage train ride tickets, then get in line for the steamer train, then ride the speeder if you're tall enough. Ride the vintage train and leave by noon or 1 p.m. to avoid the crowds and visit the fish hatchery one mile east of town, turning right at Fish Hatchery Road.

During the year, go on themed trips like "Polar Express", Halloween, and Murder Mystery Dinner Trains. Sunset Magazine rated this town as one of "The West's Best Cities". You can check out Fillmore Fish Hatchery P.O. Box 666, Fillmore, California 93016 or email fillmore@dfg.ca.gov Besides trout you might see drooling Snowy Egrets, Black-Crowned Night Herons, Mallards, Brewer's Blackbirds, and White-Faced Ibis!

You can enter the re-created Chumash buildings!

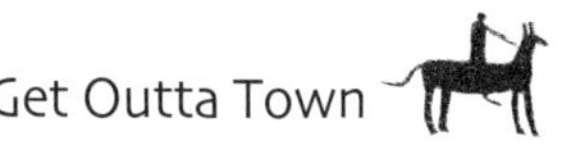

Chumash Interpretive Center (Thousand Oaks)

Rating: A for educational in history, culture, archaeology
Ages: Even pre-school children can appreciate it
Directions: 101 South 52 miles, exit Highway 23 North, go 2.8 miles and exit Avenida de los Arboles. Turn right onto E Avenida de los Arboles 1.4 miles, turn right onto N. Westlake Blvd. 0.1 mile, and left onto Lang Ranch Parkway 0.3 mile.
Contact: 492-8076 or www.chumashcenter.org
Season: Any, and it's usually about 15 degrees warmer than Santa Barbara

Tip: Call for reservations: 1 p.m. Saturdays docent-lead walk.

Oakbrook Park Chumash Interpretive Center and Museum is in a canyon and has a re-created Chumash village with homes, cemetery, two sweat lodges and a game field. There is a Chumash *tomol*, or wooden-plank canoe replica, out in front. This is well worth the drive. If at least six people reserve, there are guided nature walks Saturdays at 1 p.m., that tour the village and the cave, which contains ancient pictographs. There are a lot of oak trees, so the flat trail is shady in parts.

You can easily take a stroller all the way up the canyon since the trail is so flat and has no rocks on it. You might bring hats!

There is a good playground adjacent so youngsters can actively play after the educational visit. Bring a picnic for the canyon or the playground. Dogs, bikes, and motorized vehicles are not allowed.

Dream you're an Olympic skater at Channel Islands Ice Center.

Channel Islands Ice Center (Oxnard)

Rating: A if you like to try new sports and challenges
Ages: 9 and up; use your discretion
Directions: 101 South 37 miles; immediately after the long bridge over Santa Clara River, exit Ventura Road, at the foot of the off-ramp, continue stright through the signal light into Wagon Wheel Plaza, at 830 Wagon Wheel Road in Oxnard. It's directly across the street from the offramp.
Contact: 988-4440 or www.channelislandsice.com
Season: Mondays through Saturdays Noon-5. Sundays 10:30-5. Thursdays 7:30 p.m.-9:30 p.m also. Fridays and Saturdays 7:30 p.m.-11 p.m also.

Tip: Bring long pants, sweaters, mittens, and hats! Before your return home, ask for clear directions to 101 North!

If you're tired of warm weather, or you would like a holiday-season event, head to the air-conditioned ice and imagine you're outside on a frozen pond. Even if you don't like it, you can always grab a hot chocolate and a chocolate chip cookie and enjoy the view of skaters whizzing by in varying degrees of proficiency.

Ice skating can be a real test of your coordination, balance and adventurous spirit. This is a "broaden your horizons" type activity. It's not a cake walk, but you might be surprised how well you and your loved ones handle it. If you're the parent and you're not a decent skater, and your child falls while holding your hand, you will probably fall too. Beware. Ice is a very hard surface! Ask about youth classes.

Skate rental is extra. Ask about their "Cheap Skate" which includes skate rental and is from 10:30 a.m. to 12:30 p.m. Sundays. Call to verify hours before you go.

If you feel like you want to splurge, you can rent out the whole ice for a party of ice hockey, skating, or broomball!

Solvang's windmill: something completely different!

Solvang/Old Mission Santa Inés (Valley)

Rating: A for shopping, Danish, pastries, windmills, ice cream
Ages: All ages
Directions: 101 North 4 miles, exit Highway 154, go 24 miles and turn left on Highway 246 West to Solvang
Contact: (800) 468-6765 or www.solvangusa.com
Season: Any. It's decorated late November through the holidays

Tip: Remember it's usually warmer, sunnier, and drier here.

Highway 246 West runs smack into this city of windmills and Danish-looking architecture. It's Santa Barbara's Disneyland – without the rides. Visit Hans Christian Andersen Museum, open daily at 1680 Mission Drive, or 688-2052. The story teller was Denmark's most famous person. If you like shopping and knickknacks, you'll love it here! Or if you even like a pastry and cup of java or hot cocoa, it's an excursion destination with many nearby attractions. McConnell's Ice Cream is at 1588 Mission Street (also called Highway 246) in Solvang, 688-9880. Try pumpkin-hunting September 30-October 31 on Highway 246 just past (west of) Solvang on the right; you can get lost in a great corn maze and/or pick out a pumpkin or bizarre gourd. Year-round you can take a glider ride (see Splurge! Chapter, *Flying High*).

Shortly before you reach Solvang, look to the left and you'll see Old Mission Santa Inés, the 19th Mission, built in 1804 to be a one-day trip from the Missions in Lompoc and Santa Barbara. There are picnic tables and restrooms in the back. It's open daily 9-5:30 except Christmas and Thanksgiving at 1760 Mission Drive (Highway 246), office@missionsantaines.org or 688-4815.

Red Rock has beautiful green pools of water.

Santa Ynez Recreation Area (Paradise Road)

Rating: A for accessibility, nature, hikes, non-commercial, inexpensive
Ages: All
Directions: 101 North 4 miles, exit Highway 154, go 10 miles and turn right on Paradise Road for Santa Ynez Recreation Area, Santa Barbara Ranger District and Red Rock at the very end, 8.5 miles out.
Contact: 968-6640 or www.fs.fed.us/r5/lospadres/ or Santa Barbara Ranger District is at 3505 Paradise Road, or 967-3481 for information on water or crowd conditions
Season: The Ranger District is open 8 a.m.-4:30 p.m. daily.

Tip: Bring swimsuits, water socks and insect repellent during warm months. The 2007 Zaca Fire did not burn everything! The Paradise Road area was untouched.

If Santa Barbara is chilly or overcast in the Spring, Summer or Autumn and you feel like a swim or a good hike, this is the call. Santa Barbara's backcountry has green water pools, warm days, great trails, wildflowers, wildlife and usually sunny skies. And it's so accessible by car! Take a morning, afternoon or full day to drive out Paradise Road to investigate Santa Ynez Recreation Area. Bring a picnic lunch and just explore. During cooler months, the high waters of Santa Ynez River make it impossible to drive to the end of the road, so you'll have fewer options at that time of year. If you can't or don't want to cross the river, there are five areas along Paradise Road to park and swim or fish. Three have picnic areas and two have turnouts.

In summer, the river is easily crossed by sedan. After the rains cease and the river level drops, there's a whole new world back there. The turnout called Sandstone by locals is designated by the giant rock face across from the road. Buy an Adventure Pass for parking in lots or along the side of Paradise Road, at Big 5 Sporting Goods, 964-4749. (Exit Highway 154, turn right onto State Street and the second driveway on the right is Big 5). Or you can get a pass, as well as maps, at the Ranger District supervisor's office at 6755 Hollister, Suite 150, in Goleta.

The road ends after 8.5 miles at Red Rock parking lot. Take the trailhead by the bathroom about 20 minutes, ford the river, and continue up the trail a couple more minutes to the large green pool at the big tall Red Rock.

Two-site Cachuma Campground is adjacent to a creek.

Figueroa Mountain (Valley)

Rating: A for educational, nature, quiet, non-commercial
Ages: All
Directions: For the real wilderness, 101 North 4 miles, exit Highway 154, go 22 miles and turn right on Armour Ranch Road. Go 1.3 miles and turn right on Happy Canyon Road. Stay straight and it becomes Figueroa Mountain Road ending at Nira Campground and the doorway to trails into San Rafael Wilderness. From Santa Barbara it takes about 80 minutes to get to Nira.
Contact: 968-6640 or www.fs.fed.us/r5/lospadres/ or Santa Barbara Ranger District is at 3505 Paradise Road, or 967-3481
Season: Spring and late fall are best. Flies and heat in warmer months. It gets cold in cooler months

Tip: Buy an Adventure Pass for parking near Figueroa Mountain, at Big 5 Sporting Goods, 964-4749. (Exit Highway 154, turn right onto State Street and the second driveway on the right is Big 5). Or you can get a pass, as well as maps, at the Ranger District supervisor's office at 6755 Hollister, Suite 150, in Goleta.

This is God's country, up in the mountains. People come out here for hiking, swimming, trout fishing, birding, hunting, target shooting, off-highway vehicle tracks, and mountain biking.

It's called Santa Barbara's Back Country, as opposed to the front country of trails on the ocean side of our coastal mountains.

Figueroa Mountain Recreational Area in Los Padres National Forest is largely covered with heavy chaparral. The trails and creeks at Davy Brown, Fir Canyon and Manzana have water all year. Early wildflower blooms begin in late March with filaree and purple shooting stars. If you're looking to fish from March to mid-May, the California Department of Fish and Game stocks trout then, so Davy Brown Creek below the campground, and Manzana Creek are the place to go.

En route from Santa Barbara, the middle part of the drive has beautiful horse farms and vineyards. Just go and explore. You might spend a day driving out for a picnic and see what interests you before you come back more focused.

Ponies smaller than a little girl live at Quicksilver Ranch.

Quicksilver Ranch (Valley)

Rating: A for darling, cute, different, quiet, educational
Ages: 4-9 ideally but use your judgment with your child
Directions: 101 North 4 miles, exit Highway 154, go 24 miles and turn left on Highway 246 West. Turn right onto Alamo Pintado Road at a stop sign at the Texaco Station, and about two miles north on the left you'll see the ponies and well-marked entrance at 1555 Alamo Pintado Road
Contact: 686-4002
Season: There are usually babies in April and May. The ranch is open daily 10-3. Tours are available by appointment only for a minimum of 20 people at $3.00 per person by calling 686-4002 or emailing qsminis@syv.com

Tip: Should be combined with another valley activity nearby.

These ponies are adorable to look at, and perfect for young children to see. It can be one of your stops during a daytrip to Santa Ynez Valley. If you have visitors from out of town and they've seen enough of Santa Barbara, this is a different addition to a valley tour. Owners Aleck and Louise Stribling have bred miniature horses since 1983 and have won national championships. They breed and train 25-30 foals a year. The animals are smaller than some dogs and very gentle and patient. They are just to look at and not for riding. It's a 45-minute drive from downtown Santa Barbara, but a world away.

Flag Is Up Farms offers quiet teaching moments.

Flag Is Up Farms (Valley)

Rating: A for World Class Act, humane, quiet, animal lovers
Ages: All ages watch; it's just for viewing. Riding not available.
Directions: 101 North 4 miles, exit Highway 154, go 24 miles turn left on Highway 246 West. Go past Solvang 1.2 miles to the gates of 901 East Highway 246 on the right. About 45 minutes from Santa Barbara
Contact: 688-4382 or www.montyroberts.com
Season: Call for schedules

Tip: It's not a show; it's a working facility that you can watch in action.

Monty Roberts, "The Horse Whisperer", has his home and horse-training farm here with his wife, Pat.

Now world famous, he grew up in a violent home and was beaten so severely he had broken bones and spinal injuries. After seeing other trainers take 4-6 weeks to "break" a horse, he identified with the horses and learned to posture with his body, head and eyes to communicate with horses. He named this new language Equus.

He tames a horse that has never had a saddle on its back into accepting a saddle and rider without the use of physical force - all in less than an hour. He has even trained horses for the Queen of England!

Nojoqui Falls: a beautiful short walk even in dry season!

Nojoqui Falls County Park (Valley)

Rating: A for outdoorsy, easy, beautiful, good picnic destination
Ages: 3-up
Directions: 101 North 4 miles, exit Highway 154, go 24 miles and turn left on Highway 246 West. In Solvang turn left onto Alisal Road for 10 minutes and you'll see it on your left.
Contact: 934-6123
Season: 8 a.m. to sunset. Springtime is best season since after the rains, the waterfall flows best

Tip: Combine it with Ostrich Land 686-9696!

Say *Naw-HOE-wee*. It's about a 50-minute drive and a half-mile walk to a 163-foot waterfall named after Naxuwi, a Chumash village that was once nearby. This is a bit of a drive from Santa Barbara, but for little ones, it's the easiest access to a waterfall in Southern California! The pool isn't very deep and the bottom is rocky, but adventurous little ones have climbed behind the falls! Story has it that a drought-stricken Chumash people's leader held an all-night prayer vigil and in the morning was led to a fern grotto here by a beautiful female apparition. When she ascended, her clothes transformed into a sparkling year-round waterfall.

The park has playground equipment and picnic tables. It has been called "The Yosemite of Santa Barbara County." If you continue driving past the park two miles, you'll hit 101 South and it's 45 minutes back to Santa Barbara. Or you can take 101 North a couple miles, exit Highway 246 East, turn right and go one mile, and dine at A.J. Spurs Restaurant (see entry later in this chapter).

Feeding birds that are eight feet tall at Ostrich Land!

Ostrich Land (Valley)

Rating: A for strange, educational, unique, funny, memorable
Ages: All
Directions: 101 North 4 miles, exit Highway 154, go 24 miles and turn left on Highway 246 West. Pass Solvang and it will be on your left at 610 E. Highway 246 in Buellton
Contact: 686-9696.
Season: You might call to verify the gift shop is open

Tip: Bring your camera or video cam

How many other places can you check out ostriches up to 9 feet tall and 350 pounds on the other side of the fence? They can run 45 miles per hour and they'll eat out of your cup. There's no other bird in the world with only two toes! One egg equals about 24 chicken eggs. The mother hens incubate the eggs during the day and the father sits on the eggs at night. An ostrich chick grows one foot taller each month. The ostrich is native to Africa. Ostrich farming started in South Africa in 1857. At Ostrich Land you can buy ostrich oil, ostrich jerky, ostrich feathers, hollowed-out ostrich eggs, and ostrich meat, which is very low fat red meat, tasting like beef. You can also feed the ostriches, but you better hold on tight to the cup of meal or they'll take it out of your hand! You can also see many Emus (the national bird of Australia) which look like "tiny" six-foot ostriches.

Eat everything on your plate? Then pick a treasure from the chest.

A.J. Spurs Restaurant (Valley)

Rating: A for family-style dining, casual, multiple courses, kid-friendly
Ages: All ages
Directions: 101 North 4 miles, exit Highway 154, go 24 miles and turn left on Highway 246 West. Pass Solvang and it's on your left at 350 E. Highway 246 in Buellton
Contact: 686-1655
Season: It opens at 5 p.m. Monday through Friday; at 4 p.m. Saturday and Sunday, and closes at 9:30 p.m. every day of the year.

Tip: You can also access it via 101 north about 40 minutes, exit Highway 246, turn right, go one mile and it's on your right.

The classic (if not overdone) Western-style family restaurant, complete with stuffed full-size buffalo and polar bear! There's so much to see! It's the building with the covered wagon on the roof, in case you can't find it. Meals include soup of the day, salad, entrée, dessert, and a trip to the treasure chest for young'uns who have finished their dinner. Weekday specials are available before 6 p.m. It's very kid-friendly and should be seriously considered as the finishing touch to any day-trip to the Valley. It's a fun atmosphere inside.

"I bet you can't eat just one!"

Apple Lane Farm (Valley)

Rating: A+ for delicious, educational, cheap and fun
Ages: 4 and up
Directions: 101 North 4 miles, exit Highway 154 North. Go 24 miles and turn left on Highway 246. Turn right at the stop sign at the Texaco Station, Alamo Pintado. About a mile on your right is Apple Lane Orchards.
Contact: 688-5481
Season: Seven days a week, 10 a.m.-5 p.m., August 15 through day before Thanksgiving.

Tip: Ask for Peggy Lane's apple crisp recipe!

There is something magic about picking your own fresh crisp apples. Gala in August. Golden Delicious and Red Delicious all September and early October. Fuji in October. Granny Smith in October and November. Management charges by the bag that they provide.

This is a hobby for management. They love group tours. Call ahead to arrange a date and time. Some years, the farm closes earlier in the season – depending on the apple crop.

The magic of camping: warming up before making s'mores!

Camping With the Stars!

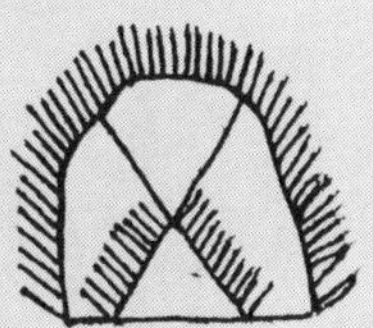

"Look deep into nature, and then you will understand everything better."
– Albert Einstein

There's something for everyone who goes camping around Santa Barbara, just like there's a top for every pot. You can enjoy clean sheets in a rental canvas tent, sleep in a creek-side cabin with a gas-log fireplace and a Jacuzzi bathtub, or backpack two miles into a protected wilderness area and see no one for 24 hours!

Don't like to cook? You can buy hot meals prepared for you.

Tired of standard camping? You can sleep in a Yurt.

Think it's too far to drive? Try camping inside City Limits!

You can backpack and camp in solitude, or drive up to a beachfront camp site amidst 100+ other camp sites.

You don't have a backpack? Rent one at Mountain Air Sports!

Don't like to set up a tent? Rent one already set up! Or you can rent a Recreational Vehicle (RV) with a kitchenette; check out (800) 671-8042 or www.cruiseamerica.com. Don't rent the movie *RV* before you go!

There are four broad categories to choose from:

※ Rental cabins, tents and yurts at Cachuma Lake County Park or El Capitan Canyon.

※ A national park typically provides your nicest scenery. Our closest national park across the channel is even surrounded by Channel Islands National Marine Sanctuary!

※ State campgrounds at Carpinteria, El Capitan and Refugio offer reservations at nice facilities for RV/car/bike/tent campers

※ Santa Barbara County parks are sometimes first-come, first served; reservations are not always allowed.

As you go, remember to respect others, their camp sites, and quiet time. Every visitor is there simply to relax or play hard, and enjoy making lifetime memories!

Visitors disembark at Scorpion Anchorage on Santa Cruz Island.

Channel Islands National Park

Rating: A for educational, conservation, boating, wildlife
Ages: Even three-year olds can camp the east end of Santa Cruz
Directions: Reserve transportation first. Reserve camping: (877) 444-6777
Contact: For boat transportation, contact:
- Condor Cruises in Santa Barbara, 965-1985 or www.condorcruises.com
- Island Packers in Ventura, 642-1393 or wwwislandpackers.com

For general information, contact
- www.nps.gov
- Visitors Center in Ventura, 658-5730
- "Outdoors Santa Barbara" visitors center, located in the Santa Barbara Maritime Museum building at 113 Harbor Way is a Channel Island information center and has an excellent map, 884-1475 or www.outdoorsb.noaa.gov.

Season: September/October are the best months as they are the lease windy. Bring thick wetsuits to swim or snorkel!

The shortest boat trip to camp on Anacapa Island is 11 miles from Channel Islands Harbor in Oxnard. It takes just over an hour. On a day trip, you can easily see East Anacapa Island, where the 8-site campground is located. There is a ranger residence, lighthouse and foghorn, water reservoir, weekend ranger-guided tour, great view of the other islands and coreopsis blooming in spring. High cliffs on all shores limit your activities, however fewer visitors come here than to Santa Cruz east end. You can't visit Middle Anacapa or West Anacapa islands unless you have a kayak and are a very experienced kayaker.

Camping Santa Cruz Island east end is best for parents with little ones and first-timers. The campground is a ten-minute walk from the dock. There is snorkeling, hiking, birding, swimming, kayak rentals and beach combing.

Santa Rosa Island camp sites all have wind breaks, and are about a ten-minute walk from the beach at Bechers Bay. There is fishing, birding, hiking and swimming.

Also windy, San Miguel Island has caliche forests and pinnepeds.

Remote Santa Barbara Island is 38 miles out from Santa Monica, and some call it "The Galapagos of California" because of its pinnepeds. It's like a one-mile raised atoll, bleak until you put your snorkel or scuba gear on.

Cachuma Lake has cabins, and even lake-view yurts!

Cachuma Lake Recreation Area

Rating: B for no lake swimming, no kayaking, no water-skiing.
Ages: All ages
Directions: 101 North 4 miles, exit Highway 154, go 17 miles and it's on your right.
Contact: 686-5054 or www.sbparks.org
Season: Hot days are hotter, and cool nights are colder over the hill.

Tip: Sleep in a lakefront yurt!

Cachuma Lake offers boat rentals, fishing, hiking, lake cruises, and a playground. People come from miles away for its bass fishing.

A different approach to camping is sleeping in a yurt with canvas walls and roof! You can watch the sun set over the lake from your yurt!

The Family Fun Center is open daily in summer and includes a swimming pool, video games, miniature golf and a snack bar. The two-hour lake cruise with a naturalist focuses on bald eagles in winter, and wildlife, wildflowers and birds during warmer months. It's appropriate for children as young as five (younger if they are patient and can be still and quiet). Walking around on the boat is prohibited.

Cabins with kitchenettes are available at 934-1441 or www.centralcoastcabins.com. Even dogs are welcome at Cachuma Lake County Park!

The World's Safest Beach boasts camp sites on the sand.

Carpinteria Beach State Park

Rating: A for probably the warmest campground near Santa Barbara
Ages: All
Directions: 101 South 10 miles, exit Linden, right at stop onto Linden, left onto Carpinteria Avenue, then right on Palm Avenue to the end of the road.
Contact: Info at 684-2811 or 566-4984 or www.reserveamerica.com or if you're calling between two days and seven months in advance, call (800) 444-7275. Also www.parks.ca.gov/?_page_ID=599
Season: Reservations required except for low season.

Tip: This is urban camping; you can walk to restaurants and shops.

"The World's Safest Beach" has long ago lost its pier, but its mile-long white sandy beach features a sea lion rookery to the south (December through May) and good hikes and mountain biking south of the park along the bluffs, if you get tired of the beach.

There is also swimming, surf fishing, surfing, tide pooling by the "tar pits" and beachcombing. If you walk to the north end of Sandyland Road, north of the park, you'll find Carpinteria Salt Marsh, where there are docent-led tours Saturdays at 10 a.m.

Also north of the park are rafts offshore that you can swim out to, and relax on, during summer months.

Children love to bike around the campground. There isn't much privacy and the camp sites are pretty small, but it has the most sites adjacent to the sand with ocean views. You need to reserve those for warmer months way in advance, or without much notice during colder months. Night trains can seem like they're coming through your tent. No need for pesky cooking! You can walk to Rusty's for pizza, or The Spot for a cheeseburger dinner and a chocolate-dipped Frosty, then in the morning, Esau's Restaurant or Cajun Kitchen for breakfast. And it's all totally legal! Who said camping had to be "roughing it?"

El Capitan is the most wooded campground and has bike trails.

El Capitan State Beach

Rating: A+ for largest camp sites around Santa Barbara
Ages: All
Directions: 101 North 20 miles, exit El Capitan State Beach Road
Contact:
www.parks.ca.gov/default.asp?page_ID=601
(800) 444-PARK www.reserveamerica.com
Season: Reservations required except for low season

Tip: Winter storms seasonally eliminate beaches.

This is the oceanfront campground for you, if you like a big, wooded camp site. Since there are so many trees, only a few camp sites have good ocean views. The attraction is more about the cozy wooded area and campground than the beach. The camp sites closest to the beach are the quietest, whereas the campsites closest to the trestle are probably the loudest. Camp site 48 is quietest from train noises and has a great tree to climb for little ones.

In Winter, the beach can be non-existent when storms take away all the sand! Surf-fish, bike, surf or go tide-pooling at the point at low tide. In Summer, you can include swimming and beach combing as well.

If you can rock-hop, start in the creek near the railroad trestle and go downstream to the beach!

Bring bikes and a picnic lunch and pedal the paved bike trail 2.5 miles north to Refugio State Beach.

You can also walk or pedal uphill and under the freeway to El Capitan Canyon for Saturday blues and jazz concerts/barbecues from April to October. That's also a good destination when it's cold or windy; you can explore the creek and the canyon.

During big surf in winter, the surf spot at the river-mouth attracts scores of surfers. If all coastal campgrounds are full, generally you can go online and get an "overflow" camp site in the group area.

If you need a snack bar or supplies, go two miles north to Refugio State Beach.

Enjoy the creek right near your cabin!

El Capitan Canyon & Ocean Mesa Campground

Rating: A for deluxe fun in cabins, tenting and Recreational Vehicle camp sites
Ages: All ages, but there are no pets allowed
Directions: US 101 North 20 miles, exit El Capitan State Beach Road, turn right into El Capitan Canyon
Contact: El Capitan Canyon (private campground), 685-3887, (866) 352-2729 or www.elcapitancanyon.com
Season: Any; cabins are fine in the rain!

Tip: For lowest rates, maximum value would be to find a warm couple of days mid-week during off-season.

For campers and non-campers, this is the far end of the spectrum; the camping polar opposite of backpacking. This canyon is inland from the El Capitan Beach State Park, the railroad tracks, and the freeway, and it offers "amenities that pamper" such as a spa, heated pool, laundry facilities, ATM, Internet access, TV, and cabins complete with Jacuzzis, fireplaces, full bathrooms, linens, towels and kitchenettes. The cabins are actually trailers made to look like cabins. There are also walk-in canvas tent-cabins. You can rent a creek-side cabin with a loft for the little ones but it may be at Splurge! chapter prices.

There are daytime crafts programs for children, if parents would like a free moment for a professional massage treatment. You can bring your car to your cabin to unpack, but you return to the parking lot at the entrance so the canyon remains "car free." No pets.

The creek provides hours of fun for youngsters, whether it's rock-hopping or searching for polliwogs. There are also hiking trails, horses to ride, and a limited number of complimentary bicycles. The beach is a 10-25 minute walk away, depending on how far up the canyon you are.

The blues and jazz concerts start at 6 p.m. Saturdays from April to October. There is a cover charge per person and the optional barbecue dinner is additional.

The market sells organic groceries, sandwiches, and wine.

A new addition is Ocean Mesa Campground, opened in 2006, with 80 RV camp sites and 20 tent camp sites, all with access to El Capitan Canyon amenities. The campground provides ocean-view campsites.

Surfers enjoy Hobson County Beach too.

Hobson County Beach

Rating: B- for scant beach and adjacent to Pacific Coast Highway
Ages: All
Directions: 101 South 18 miles, exit Seacliff, turn right onto Pacific Coast Highway 0.5 mile, to 5210 W. Pacific Coast Highway. It's about 19 miles from Garden Street.
Season: No reservations allowed; first-come, first-served to secure a camp site
Contact: 654-3951 or http://gsa.countyofventura.org/parks/parkinfo.htm and click on "Visiting."

Tip: There's only sandy beach at lower tides.

If you (A) don't need much or any beach adjacent to the campground, and (B) you simply want the salty scent of the sea, this ocean-front Ventura County Park has 31 camp sites for you, shoe-horned into a tiny lot without serious vegetation. You can only see the water from atop the boulders.

It's best for those with trailers or campers. It's sandwiched between Pacific Coast Highway and large rocks keeping out the Pacific Ocean. On the other side of Pacific Coast Highway are the railroad tracks.

There is a beach only at the lowest tides. It's most ideal for fishing, surfing and winter tide pooling. There are no parking places or picnic tables for day users.

This has more play area and is safer for youngsters than Rincon Parkway to the south, but there isn't much to do if the beach is under water or rocky. This, and Rincon Parkway are NOT recommended for those with youngsters that might wander onto Pacific Coast Highway or the railroad tracks.

You can always drive a mile north on Pacific Coast Highway and take your last left under the freeway (before it dead-ends) to a nice sandy beach to play and swim, if you want a white-sand beach.

This campground is for those who can't get in anywhere else, and simply must be at the coast.

Rincon Parkway has 127 camp sites right on the ocean and the highway.

Rincon Parkway Parking Meter Zone

Rating: B- for no vegetation, highway-side parking
Ages: Only go here if your children won't wander onto the highway
Directions: 101 South 18 miles, exit Seacliff, turn right onto Pacific Coast Highway 1.5 miles, to just south of 5210 W. Pacific Coast Highway. It's about 19.5 miles from Garden Street.
Season: No reservations allowed; first-come, first-served to secure a parking place
Contact: 654-3951 or http://gsa.countyofventura.org/parks/parkinfo.htm and click on "Visiting."

Tip: You must have a Recreational Vehicle to park here.

This is a great parking zone (it's not a campground) if you have a Recreational Vehicle. It's for those who enjoy parking on Pacific Coast Highway, between the railroad tracks and the ocean.

There are 127 parking places with asphalt to park on and pitch tents on (if you have sleeping pads!), and boulders to protect you from the waves, and that's about it! You can't see much of the water without climbing a rock.

Activities include hiking/beachcombing at the lowest tides, surfing, and surf fishing. Medium and high tides leave little or no beach. If you want a beach, you can always drive two miles north on PCH and take your last left under the freeway before PCH dead-ends, to a no-name white sandy beach.

Walking or biking on adjacent Pacific Coast Highway 10 feet from your vehicle is not advisable. Cars zoom by at 50+ miles per hour. This is not ideal for children. No picnicking. The restrooms are portable toilets. Hobson to the north and Faria to the south are preferable, but still not ideal.

If you remove your Recreational Vehicle from your parking place, you're giving it up, the supervisor says. Your vehicle parked in your parking place, with a receipt on the dashboard, secures your parking place. You can't "save" a space.

Only dolphins and surfers enjoy the surf at Faria.

Faria County Beach

Rating: B- for tiny camp sites, scant vegetation
Ages: All
Directions: 101 South 18 miles, exit Seacliff, turn right onto Pacific Coast Highway 2.5 miles, to 4350 W. Pacific Coast Highway. It's about 21 miles from Garden Street.
Season: No reservations allowed; first-come, first-served to secure a camp site
Contact: 654-3951 or http://gsa.countyofventura.org/parks/parkinfo.htm and click on "Visiting."

Tip: There is sandy beach in summer only at the lowest tides.

The 42 sites packed in here are best for those with RVs or a jones to be near the ocean.

The shore here is typically rocky. There are no easy ways in or out of the water.

Amenities include a playground, horseshoe pits, and a snack bar. There are a couple of trees, but generally no privacy.

At the lowest tides, you can go beachcombing or tide pooling. This campground is like Rincon Parkway and Hobson in that giant boulders separate you from the ocean, although this campground is a little quieter, since it is below Pacific Coast Highway. This is not for those campers whose children might wander up onto the highway or railroad tracks across the highway.

Faria is the closest campground to Mando's – a surf spot for the beginning surfer who likes long, gentle waves. Mando's is about 0.5 mile south, just after the long row of houses immediately south of Faria.

Beachcombers enjoy low-tide Refugio.

Refugio State Beach

Rating: A for white sandy beach, palm trees, quiet cove, creek
Ages: All
Directions: 101 North 22 miles, exit Refugio Road
Contact: Info at http://www.parks.ca.gov/default.asp?page_id=603. Or to reserve: or www.reserveamerica.com or (800) 444-PARK two days to seven months in advance
Season: Reservations required except for low season.

Tip: Even seven-year-olds can ride horses nearby!

This is Santa Barbara's little slice of Hawaii, but its beginnings were wild.

This is where Hippolyte de Bouchard the pirate, who raided the Santa Barbara Channel during the 1800s, stopped after looting the village of Monterey up north. Three of the fearsome French captain's pirates were captured by soldiers from the Presidio, trying to steal supplies and food from the ranchos on the mainland. Bouchard left for more supplies at Santa Cruz Island, then returned four days later; his 285 men threatened bloodshed against the 50 soldiers. The soldiers tricked the pirates into thinking there were more soldiers, and the pirates negotiated peacefully for their captured comrades, and left.

Today you can ride, instead of raid. Pedal the paved bike path 2.5 miles south along the coast to El Capitan State Beach. Or swim, snorkel, fish, hike, surf, kayak, or simply relax under the magnificent palm trees lining the wind-sheltered white sand beach. Refugio Creek bisects the park. The headland acts as a good shelter from the prevailing winds. There is an excellent picnic area on the grass under the palm trees, adjacent to the cove near the point. Horseback riding for children seven years old and up is five minutes away – up Refugio Road at Circle Bar B Stables. Bring your kayak if you have one!

At minus tides you can go tide-pooling at the point. There's enough of a hill at the point that passing southbound freight trains put on screechy brakes, especially noticeable during the night. It's best to get camp sites nearest the water and toward the south end of the camp ground. There's a snack bar during summer.

Paradise Road pavement crosses Santa Ynez River repeatedly.

Santa Ynez Recreation Area

Santa Barbara Ranger District, Los Padres National Forest

Rating: B- for beautiful and close, but flies and crowds
Ages: All
Directions: 101 North 4 miles, exit 154 North 10 miles, turn right onto Paradise Road. There are about five campgrounds on both sides of the road.
Contact: Information at 968-6640/967-8766 or www.fs.fed.us/r5/lospadres/ or Santa Barbara Ranger District is at 3505 Paradise Road / 967-3481. Reservations at www.reserveamerica.com
Season: Autumn is best, spring is second, summer has flies, winter can be cold.

Tip: Visit all campgrounds to see which you prefer before planning a camp out.

The great thing about these five campgrounds near Santa Ynez River is that they allow you to get out of town for even one night and be back in time for church or soccer games the next day! These are the campgrounds to head to when you have no time for a long road trip and you just want to camp.

The mileage from Highway 154 at Paradise Road is 7.3 to Sage Hill Campground, 7.7 to Los Prietos Campground, 7.8 to Paradise Campground, 8.0 to Fremont Campground and 8.4 to Upper Oso Campground. Reservations are required except there are a few first-come first-served sites that fill up quickly during peak season. Fremont Campground and Los Prietos Campground are closed from October 30 until March 30. During that time, you can use Upper Oso Campground, Paradise Campground, or if you're a larger group, Sage Hill Campground, which is perfect because you can't see any other camp sites, it's near the river, and it's near a trailhead.You can book online, or just chance it and drive there to see what's open.

These campgrounds are good for biking, hiking, fishing, sunbathing, and swimming. Or just relaxing in camp!

Trout are planted in the spring. Sometimes during warmer months, pesky flies can be a bother unless you have an RV or walk-in tent with a screen.

Spring is good since it's greener, there are fewer flies, there's more water in the river, and it's not as crowded. During the rainy season, you may have to call a day before to verify the river is passable with your vehicle!

Lost Valley Campground is a perfect destination for youth backpackers.

Figueroa Mountain Recreation Area

Rating: A for nature, quiet, non-commercial
Ages: All
Directions: For San Rafael Wilderness, 101 North 4 miles, exit Highway 154, go 22 miles and turn right on Armour Ranch Road. Go 1.3 miles and turn right on Happy Canyon Road. Continue on straight and it becomes Sunset Valley Road at the intersection of Figueroa Mountain Road, ending at Nira Campground and the entrance to trails into San Rafael Wilderness. From Santa Barbara it takes about 80 minutes.
Contact: 968-6640 or www.fs.fed.us/r5/lospadres/ or Santa Barbara Ranger District is at 3505 Paradise Road, or 967-3481
Season: Spring and late fall are best, and have the least visitors. The heat and flies increase in warmer months. It can even snow in winter on upper elevations.

Tip: Buy an Adventure Pass for parking around Figueroa Mountain. They're available at Big 5 Sporting Goods, 964-4749, or at the Ranger District supervisor's office, at 6755 Hollister, Suite 150, in Goleta.

Back-country mountain-type and wilderness campgrounds: **Cachuma** has 6 sites sheltered by large oaks at the bottom of a narrow canyon and is free. This is not to be confused with Cachuma Lake Campground. **Davy Brown** has 13 sites, water, and is free all year. **Figueroa** has 32 sites amongst pine and manzanita, a great view of Santa Ynez Valley, water and is open all year. **Nira** has 12 shaded sites under oak trees and is free. **Ballard** has 2 sites that are accessible by foot only.

Backpacking beginners, start at the end of the road at Nira and enter San Rafael Wilderness! Take the level Manzana Creek Trail along the creek 30 minutes to Lost Valley Campground where there's a picnic table and fire pit. Too easy? Hike 1.5 miles farther, just past where Fish Creek empties into Manzana Creek, and cross Manzana Creek to Fish Creek Campground; a two-creek place to camp.

Bring swimsuits and water socks if you want to cool off on warm days. Every successive trip you can go farther back into the wilderness as your interest/strength develops.

Skofield Park has a big lawn and some rocks to climb.

Skofield Park

Rating: A for tent camping inside City limits!
Ages: All
Directions: Call first for application and reservations
Contact: 564-5433 or www.santabarbaraca.gov and click on "Visitors."
Season: Whenever your non-profit group can get reservations

Tip: Group camping for non-profit organizations only.

This is definitely the nearest faraway place! It can handle a large number of campers. Rattlesnake Canyon Trailhead is adjacent for hiking! Go outside the park and turn left; you'll see the trailhead adjacent to a rock bridge. If you go toward mid-day, there are cool pools in the shade to soak your toes. Be sure an adult leads hikes to scout out snakes on the trail.

Youth groups that are non-profit organizations can sleep overnight here; the large grassy area is wonderful. Have a barbeque and a bonfire. The facilities are perfect for cooking and preparing food for large amounts of people. The slope of the lawn is ideal for slippery-slides!

It's amazing how warm it can be here in the foothills, even though it's just minutes from downtown. How many people can say they've camped inside Santa Barbara City limits?

From here it's a 25-minute drive to the top of East Camino Cielo with commanding views of Santa Barbara Channel and six islands on a clear day.

If you've come here to camp and have forgotten anything, you can drive to the market. If you're having a bad night's sleep, you can drive home for a good night's sleep and return for breakfast!

Six covered wagons circle a fire pit at Rancho Oso.

Rancho Oso Guest Ranch and Stables

Rating: A for outdoorsy, home cooking, and affordable
Ages: All
Directions: Call first for reservations
Contact: 683-5686 or www.rancho-oso.com
Season: Summer can be very warm; spring and fall are best

Tip: You can't use your own tent; you rent a rustic cabin or "covered wagon."

This could be the best value in the book. The facilities-per-dollar-spent ratio is excellent.

This is the place to go if you'd like to have all weekend meals cooked for you, the dishes washed and dried for you, and all at a reasonable price. Weekend meals are on red and white checkered tablecloths in the old stone lodge. Heck, you can even watch a World Series baseball game on the TV!

The public can rent tiny cabins, just big enough to sleep in.

Or you may choose replicas of covered wagons with cots inside. Be sure to bring extra blankets or sleeping bags because in effect you're sleeping outdoors while in the covered wagon. There are six covered wagons around each fire pit, so this works very well for groups. Bring lots of firewood for a bonfire after dinner.

Amenities include two pools, Jacuzzi, playground equipment, basketball court, foosball, data port, store, laundry facility, and a tennis court. You take your meals in the "Old Stone Lodge," previously a hunting lodge, where there is also a fireplace, TV and table tennis.

Horseback riding is available for anyone eight years old and up. Call ahead to reserve at 683-5110. Guests can take very short hikes to Santa Ynez River or to the waterfall. Fishing is also available.

The weekend before Halloween is special and there are many youth activities. There are festivities at other times of the year as well.

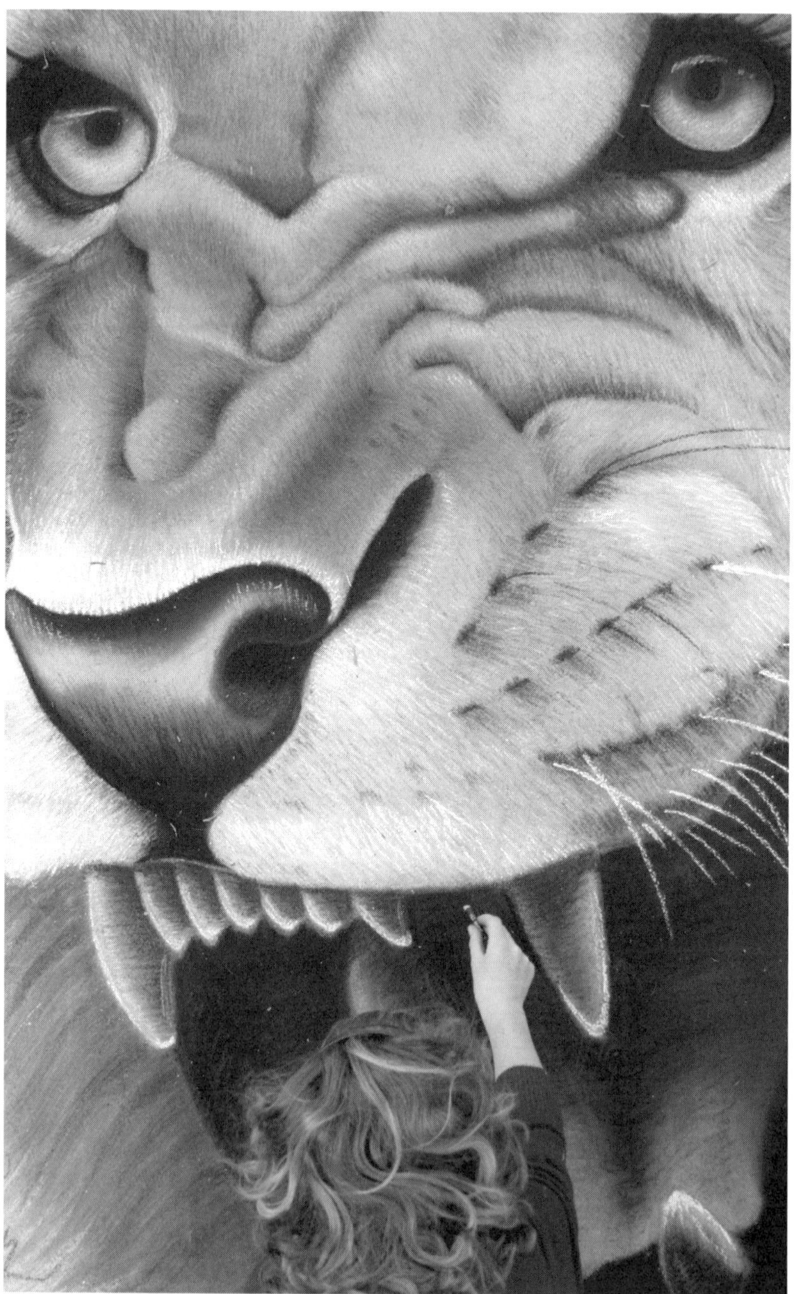

I Madonnari Festival is a street-painting event for artists and spectators.

(And Now for Something Completely Different)

Festivals and Events

Slow down and enjoy life. It's not only the scenery you miss by going too fast – you also miss the sense of where you are going and why. – Eddie Cantor

There's nothing like a special event in a special place, whether it's standing on one foot at Bourbon Street during Mardi Gras and not falling down because the crowd is so thick, or watching an impromptu Hindu Bali parade with umbrellas in a remote Indonesian village.

Some of Santa Barbara's special events are world class. For a most complete, up-to-date online calendar of events and festivals, go to www.santabarbarafun.net

A huge source of special events is UCSB, so check the calendar for the next six months at www.artsandlectures.ucsb.edu and you can buy tickets online, at the UCSB ticket office, or at 893-3535. Also check the calendar of Museum of Natural History/Sea Center at 682-4711 or www.sbnature.org. Lobero Theatre's events are at 963-0761 or www.lobero.com. You can find Arlington Theatre's events at its ticket office at 1317 State Street, 963-4408 or www.ticketmaster.com/venue/73731. Santa Barbara Museum of Art events are at 963-4364 or www.sbmuseart.org. A good general site for events is www.sbchamber.com and click on Visiting Santa Barbara, then click on Events Calendar. There are well-grounded festivals (Sand Castle Festival) to ethereal festivals (Paragliding Festival). Even if you don't like the theme, you've got to love, enjoy and admire the devotion of those involved. Some of these simply aren't to be missed!

A real child knows it doesn't matter if you say, "Happy Birthday", "Viva La Fiesta" or "Party On!", it's all about fun . . .

Year Round Free Events

Arts & Crafts Show, every Sunday, weather permitting.

Why go? This is the longest-running public weekly art show in America. It's the oldest made-locally-by-locals-and-sold-by-locals show in California! The longest-involved artists are closest to Stearns Wharf in a strictly enforced pecking order. On summer Saturdays it's whoever arrives first, sells closest to the wharf, closest to the tourists.

Directions: 101 exit Garden Street toward ocean and park.

Santa Barbara Farmers Market

Why go? Less expensive, fresher produce nearly every day of the week, weather permitting

Directions: See Farmers Market entry, Chapter 2

Contact: 962-5354 or www.sbfarmersmarket.org

Fishermen's Market

Why go? The local fishermen are so nice and the fish is so fresh. Oh yeah, their seagoing tales and the variety of sea life are also educational! 7:30 a.m.-11:30 a.m. Saturdays. If you miss it, fresh fish is available in the fish market at Harbor Way, 75 steps away.

Directions: 101 North, exit Castillo, turn left at the signal, left again under the freeway, right at the end onto Cabrillo Blvd, then first left into the harbor.

Santa Barbara Airport Tour Program

Why go? This is the home of Little Spirit, a small airplane built for children to climb into, complete with headphones! Tours can focus on aircraft design, flight instruction, weather forecasting, air traffic control, wetland ecology based on Goleta sloughs species, and the history of aviation in the region. For schools and youth organizations, Tuesday through Thursday, 9-4.

Directions: 101 North 10 miles, exit Fairview, straight through signal, up over freeway, right on Hollister, left on Lopez Rd., right on Firestone, left on Hartley Pl.

Contact: 964-7622 or www.flysb.com

Carpinteria Salt Marsh Tour

Why go? Every Saturday at 10 a.m. there are docent-led one-hour tours of a precious thing: a salt marsh. Millions drive by it, but few stop to learn; it's fascinating.

Directions: 101 South 8 miles to Linden Avenue exit, right on Linden, to Sandyland Road, right until it dead-ends into Ash Street,

and the marsh.

Contact: 684-5479 or www.cityofcarpinteria.com

Sunday Kite Fly

Why go? Every Sunday in Summer at 5 p.m., people just wanna have fun!

Directions: Garden Street exit toward ocean, right on Cabrillo Boulevard, up the hill to Shoreline Park.

Drum Circle

Why go? Drumming can be as good as a campfire; so basic!

Directions: 101 Exit Garden Street, turn toward ocean, left on Cabrillo Boulevard about 300 yards. It's 4 p.m. Saturdays when drummers and spectators congregate, see "Under Your Nose" chapter for entry.

Riding ponies rules at day-end of Triple Train Heaven, Los Angeles

The following festivals and events are listed in the approximate order in which they occur.

January

New Year's Day Hang Gliding and Paragliding Festival

Why go? If you're looking for a spectator sport other than football, January 1

Directions: 101 North five miles, exit Las Positas toward the ocean, left onto Cliff Drive, left into Elings Park South

Contact: www.flyaboveall.com

Santa Barbara International Film Festival

Why go? If you do your homework online or research in local publications, you can find educational, thoughtful and entertaining films rated "G."

Contact: 963-0023 or www.sbiif.org

February

Flying Leap Storytelling Festival

Why go? Old and young alike enjoy a good yarn…

Directions: 101 North five miles, exit Highway 154 over San Marcos Pass, left on 246 to Solvang

Contact: 688-9533 or www.solvangusa.com

Japanese Tea Ceremony

Why go? Teach about a different culture, in a nice setting.

Directions: 101 North, exit Mission toward mountains, go past the Mission to Foothill. Turn right then left at the first stop sign. Follow signs to the Botanic Garden.

Contact: 682-4726 or www.sbbg.org

Enjoy the anteater while you wait for the train! Santa Barbara Zoo.

March

Whale Festival

Why go? Not only are there music, food, and crafts in a two-day street fair, but this festival benefits the low-profile, but incredible Santa Barbara Marine Mammal Center (which shelters/cures marine mammals found on our beaches) and Channel Islands National Marine Sanctuary. There are also talks by naturalists.

Directions: Exit 101 at Garden, turn toward ocean, right at the signal onto Cabrillo. Your next signal turn left onto Stearns Wharf.

Contact: 897-3187 or www.sbwhalefestival.com

Doll Show

Why go? Your daughter will explain…

Directions: 101 North five miles, exit Las Positas, straight through signal, then right into Earl Warren Showgrounds, 10 a.m.-3 p.m.

Contact: 733-1261 or www.earlwarren.com

America's Teaching Zoo (Moorpark)

Why go? The care and training of exotic animals such as lions and hyenas occurs at Moorpark College, and the public can see the results every weekend! The big Spring Spectacular is the last two weekends of March and the first weekend of April.

Directions: 101 South about 45 minutes then 23 North to Moorpark 15 minutes, exit Collins Drive, left onto Collins Drive, right onto Campus Park Drive, left onto Campus Road and go about one-half mile to 7075 Campus Road.

Contact: 378-1441 or www.moorparkcollege.edu

March or April

Eggstraordinary bunnies and egg hunt activities usually occur the Saturday or two Saturdays before Easter Sunday, and sometimes require registration.

Botanic Garden, 682-4726 x102 or www.sbbg.org
Eggstravaganza in Buellton, 688-7529
YMCA, 687-7720
South Coast Railroad Museum, 964-3540, weekday afternoons
Calvary Chapel Concert/hunt, Easter Sunday at the Courthouse
Fillmore & Western Railway, 524-2546
Eggstravaganza at Chase Palm Park, 564-5495
Word of Life Christian service/hunt, 564-7088
Elings Park, bring your own basket, 569-5611

Feel prickly sea urchins in Ty Warner Sea Center on Stearns Wharf.

April

Earth Day Festival

Why go? There is an area specifically for children, music, organic food court and vendors. Walk, bike or take the bus there!

Directions: 101 exit Garden, turn inland until Anapamu, and turn left one block to the Santa Barbara County Courthouse Sunken Garden at Santa Barbara and Anapamu streets, 10-5:30

Contact: 963-0583 or www.communityenvironmentalcouncil.org

Sea Festival & Tall Ship Visit

Why go? Two days of history, fun, imagining the past

Directions: 101 Garden Street exit toward ocean, right on Cabrillo to the harbor

Contact: Santa Barbara Maritime Museum at 962-8404 or www.sbmm.org

Presidio Days

Why go? This is probably more pure history of Santa Barbara than the Fiesta! The beginnings of European habitation of the area is the Presidio, the fort where the Spanish first lived. There is related music and dancing, and sometimes descendants of early Spanish and Chumash inhabitants perform ceremonies.

Directions: 101 Exit Garden, turn inland to Canon Perdido Street, then turn left to 123 East Canon Perdido.

Contact: 965-0093 or www.sbthp.org

Kite Festival

Why go? It's a family-style event with games, kite flights and competition for one day.

Directions: 101 North exit Castillo, turn left at the siginal, left onto Castillo, then right onto Cliff Drive to Santa Barbara City College (past the signal) West Campus Lawn.

Contact: 682-2895x20/637-6202 or www.sbkitefest.com

Santa Barbara Fair & Expo

Why go? This is as close to a county fair as you'll get in Santa Barbara. For five days in late April, there are a lot of things geared toward children of all ages such as pony rides, puppet shows, BMX Bicycle Team, carnival rides and games

Directions: 101 North, exit Las Positas Road through signal and right into parking lot.

Contact: 687-0766 or www.earlwarren.com

Touch new things at Anacapa Island for a fascinating adventure.

Village of Tales, Ojai Storytelling Festival

Why go? The nation's best-known storytellers! Call to verify whether it will be held in April or May. It's the theater for the spoken word. It's for all ages.

Directions: 101 South 13 miles exit Highway 150 to Ojai

Contact: 646-8907 or www.ptgo.org

May

Cinco De Mayo Festival

Why go? Although September 16 is Mexico's real independence day, north of the border, the celebration is May 5, and it's big here! Dancing, music, kids corner.

Directions: 101, Exit Garden Street, turn inland to De La Guerra Street, and turn left and park. De La Guerra Plaza is between State and Anacapa streets.

Contact: 965-8561 or www.cincodemayosb.com

Mother's Day 5/10k Run and Family Festival

Why go? There is a children's fun run, and there are more than 70 vendors with crafts, touch tanks, cookie decorating, and obstacle courses. This event is based in Goleta Beach park and proceeds go to a different local non-profit organization every year.

Contact: 448-2426 or www.sbparent.com

Children's Festival

Why go? The clowns, crafts workshops, pony rides, carnival games, magicians, face painting, and music is great, and it all benefits child guidance counseling programs. 10 a.m.-4 p.m.

Directions: 101 Exit Garden, inland to Micheltorena, turn left to 1400 Alameda Park at Anacapa Street.

Contact: 965-1001 or www.fsacares.org/spotlight.htm

Family Zoo Snooze

Why go? Get night-time and morning Santa Barbara Zoo tours and sleep at the Zoo! Children must be at least five years old. Breakfast is included too!

Directions: 101 South one mile, exit Milpas St., right at signal, left after railroad tracks and you'll see the zoo on your left.

Contact: www.sbzoo.org or 962-5339. Also ask about private groups of 15.

Santa Barbara Harbor & Seafood Festival

Why go? Celebrate a good thing…

Directions: 101 Exit Garden toward ocean, right to Stearns Wharf and the harbor.

Contact: museum@sbmm.org or 962-8404 x115.

Renaissance Faire

Why go? Dress up in period 1575 garb and have complete strangers address your tiny daughter as "Princess". Jungle gym, parades, fishing. It's the nearest Renaissance Faire to Santa Barbara.

Directions: 101 South, exit Highway 150 until you see signs, it's 30 miles

Contact: 496-6036 or www.goldcoastfestivals.com

I Madonnari Festival: Chalk Painting at the Mission

Why go? Besides the music and food booths, which are reason enough, this Italian street chalking festival features serious and amateur artists creating their finest masterpieces on the asphalt. The best "paintings" are simply amazing. It's Saturday through Monday over Memorial Day Weekend, therefore the later in the weekend the more complete the "paintings" are. If you're simply interested in the art, you can always go any day following the weekend until it rains, and you'll avoid the crowds.

Directions: 101 North exit Mission Street, turn right to the Mission.

Contact: 964-4710 x4411 or www.imadonnarifestival.com

Strawberry Festival in Oxnard

Why go? Live music all day, puppet shows, magicians, clowns, music for children, and Strawberryland For Kids. This was a two-time winner of L.A. Parent Magazine's "Family Favorite Award," and it benefits more than 25 non-profit organizations.

Directions: 101 South 32 miles, exit Victoria, turn left at the signal then right onto Victoria. Go a couple miles to Channel Islands Blvd., turn left/east, follow Channel Islands Blvd. to the Festival. There will be signs to Strawberry Meadows of College Park, 3250 South Rose Avenue, Oxnard. (45 min.)

Contact: (888) 288-9242 toll free, or (805) 385-4739 or csf@strawberry-fest.org or www.strawberry-fest.org

Israel Independence Day Festival

Why go? It's a one-day festival celebrating Jewish arts, culture and heritage.

Contact: israelfestival@gmail.com

El Capitan Canyon's Summer Concerts & Barbecue

Why go? 6-9 p.m. Saturdays, barbecue dinner, outdoor setting, fun music, it's untouchable for the family! Ya gotta go! Bring sand/beach chairs, sweatshirts.

Directions: 101 North 26 miles, exit El Capitan State Beach, follow signs to El Capitan Canyon on the right

Contact: www.elcapitancanyon.com or (866) 352-2729

June whale-watching and island trips at times include dolphins off the bow.

June

Summer Thursday Concerts at Chase Palm Park

Why go? Eight Thursday evenings 6-8:30 (except for Fiesta Thursday). Bring your own lawn chair and picnic dinner. It starts on the last Thursday in June. This has to be one of Santa Barbara's premiere attractions when the evening is warm and the live band is a good one. If the little ones get bored they can always enjoy the nearby playground equipment (you'll still be able to hear the music from the playground). Music ranges from The Platters to Nouveau Flamenco, Captain Cardiac and the Coronaries, Nate Birkey Band and Elvis impersonator Raymond Michael.

Directions: Exit Garden Street towards the ocean and the only parking lots are at the corners of Cabrillo and Garden across the street from the Carousel and Chase Palm Park. Walk to the far east/south of Chase Palm Park

Contact: 897-1982 or www.sbparksandrecreation.com for calendar of bands.

Live Oak Music Festival

Why go? Three days of Father's Day weekend camping and/or non-mainstream family music with historical and cultural roots. Take 154 North over the mountain, about 35 minutes from downtown!

Contact: www.liveoakfest.org

Outdoor Concerts at Alameda Park

Why go? Nothing like a Summer Sunday outdoor concert from 1 p.m.-3 p.m. Schedules available in May. It's the oldest park in town

Directions: 101 exit Garden, inland to Sola

Contact: 897-1982 or www.sbparksandrecreation.com

Santa Barbara Bicycle Festival

Why go? Started in 2005, there have been new downhill and cross country mountain bike trails created, which are used during this festival's races. Clinics are available for children as young as 10 during the year. This festival is not only for BMX racers and spectators; there is music and food. 8 a.m.-6 p.m. $20.00 from each entry is donated to Elings Park Foundation

Directions: 101 North, exit Las Positas Road, turn toward the ocean, approximately 1 mile to the main entrance to Elings Park on the left. For the downhill racing venue, pass the main entrance, turn left on Cliff Drive. Look for the second entrance about 1/4 mile on the

A mini-matador shows poise, style and flair during summer's Fiesta Parade.

left. Park along the dirt road inside the park and wait for the shuttle.

Contact: www.santabarbarabikefest.com, www.elingspark.org

Solstice Parade and Festival

Why go? If you're not afraid of a little bawdiness, this parade can be fun.

Directions: 101 Exit Garden, turn inland. The Noon parade on Saturday near Summer Solstice is on State Street, from Cota Street to Micheltorena Street. The festival is at Alameda Park, corner of Micheltorena and Santa Barbara streets.

Contact: 965-3396 or www.solsticeparade.com

El Capitan Canyon's Summer Concerts & Barbecue

Why go? 6-9 p.m. Saturdays, Barbecue dinner, outdoor setting, fun music, it's untouchable for the family! Ya gotta go! Bring sand/beach chairs, sweatshirts.

Directions: 101 North 26 miles, exit El Capitan State Beach, follow signs to El Capitan Canyon on the right

Contact: www.elcapitancanyon.com or (866) 352-2729

Big Dog Parade & Festival

Why go? More than 2,000 dogs, some dressed in costumes, and their owners parade from De La Guerra Plaza to Chase Palm Park. Anyone can bring their dog and march in the parade. The parade ends at the Canine Festival: live music, food, dog demonstrations, games, a bounce house for children

Directions: 101 Exit Garden inland to De La Guerra, turn left.

Contact: 963-8727x1398 or www.bigdogs.com

Irish Festival

Why go? Two days of festival, celebrating Irish culture!

Directions: 101 North, exit Pueblo and turn right at the stop sign to Oak Park.

Contact: 687-4343, www.santabarbara.com/events

Lompoc Flower Festival

Why go? Four days of arts, crafts, food, parade, carnival, music, tours of the flower fields, and of course, the flower show at Veterans Memorial Building, 100 East Locust Avenue.

Directions: 101 North about 40 miles, exit Highway 1, 14 miles to Lompoc

Contact: 735-8511 or www.flowerfestival.org or www.lompoc.com

Turkeys race chuck wagons during the Ventura County Fair.

July

Summer Thursday Concerts at Chase Palm Park

Why go? Every Thursday evening 6-8:30 (except for Fiesta Thursday). Bring your own lawn chair and picnic dinner. This has to be one of Santa Barbara's premiere attractions when the evening is warm and the live band is a good one. If the little ones get bored they can always enjoy the nearby playground equipment (you'll still be able to hear the music from the playground). Music ranges from The Platters to Nouveau Flamenco, Captain Cardiac and the Coronaries, Nate Birkey Band and Elvis impersonator Raymond Michael.

Directions: Exit Garden Street towards the ocean and the only parking lots are at the corners of Cabrillo and Garden across the street from the Carousel and Chase Palm Park. Walk to the far east/south of Chase Palm Park

Contact: 897-1982 or www.sbparksandrecreation.com for calendar of bands

Outdoor Concerts at Alameda Park

Why go? Nothing like a Summer Sunday outdoor concert from 1 p.m.-3 p.m. Schedules available in May. It's the oldest park in town

Directions: 101 exit Garden, inland to Sola

Contact: 897-1928 or www.sbparksandrecreation.com

Fourth of July Parade

Why go? On State Street from Micheltorena to Cota streets, this is like a Normal Rockwell painting! Fireworks show, off main beach, 9 p.m.

Directions: 101 exit Garden inland, left to State Street

Contact: 961-2556 or www.spiritof76sb.org

Fourth of July Concert

Why go? If your child can appreciate it, Santa Barbara Symphony plays in the Courthouse Sunken Garden at 5 p.m. on July 4. Free.

Directions: 101, exit Garden St., inland to Anapamu, left to the courthouse.

Contact: www.thesymphony.org

Zoovies

Why go? What's better than an outdoor movie at the Zoo? Wednesdays 7:30 p.m. in July

Directions: 101 south exit Milpas St., turn toward the ocean. Turn left after the railroad tracks, 1/3 mile and the Zoo will be on your left.

Contact: 962-5339 or www.sbzoo.org

Feel the horsepower: driving Indy cars at Golf N' Stuff in Ventura.

French Festival

Why go? Two days, 11-7, to celebrate cuisine, culture, music, art, dancing and *joie de vivre*. Poodle parade and huge Eiffel Tower!

Directions: 101 North, exit Pueblo, right at the stop sign to Oak Park.

Contact: 564-7274 or www.frenchfestival.com

Greek Festival

Why go? It's a two-day, 11-7, cultural festival featuring Greek music, food, arts and crafts.

Directions: 101 North, exit Pueblo and turn right at the stop sign to Oak Park.

Contact: 683-4492

Semana Nautica

Why go? Is there anything funnier than cardboard kayak races? It's a sports festival, both silly and serious, for physically challenged, for amateur and professional athletes of all ages.

Directions: It depends on which of the 40 sporting events you like

Contact: 897-2680 or www.semananautica.com

El Capitan Canyon's Summer Concerts & Barbecue

Why go? 6-9 p.m. Saturdays, Barbecue dinner, outdoor setting, fun music, it's untouchable for the family! Ya gotta go! Bring sand/beach chairs, sweatshirts.

Directions: 101 North 26 miles, exit El Capitan State Beach, follow signs to El Capitan Canyon on the right

Contact: (866) 352-2729 or www.elcapitancanyon.com

Feeling the thrill of the Midway at August's Ventura County Fair.

August

Summer Thursday Concerts at Chase Palm Park

Why go? Every Thursday evening 6-8:30 (except for Fiesta Thursday). Bring your own lawn chair and picnic dinner. This has to be one of Santa Barbara's premiere attractions when the evening is warm and the live band is a good one. If the little ones get bored they can always enjoy the nearby playground equipment (you'll still be able to hear the music from the playground). Music ranges from The Platters to Nouveau Flamenco, Captain Cardiac and the Coronaries, Nate Birkey Band and Elvis impersonator Raymond Michael.

Directions: Exit Garden Street towards the ocean and the only parking lots are at the corners of Cabrillo and Garden across the street from the Carousel and Chase Palm Park. Walk to the far east/south of Chase Palm Park

Contact: 897-1982 or www.sbparksandrecreation.com for calendar of bands

Outdoor Concerts at Alameda Park

Why go? Nothing like a Summer Sunday outdoor concert from 1 p.m.-3 p.m. Schedules available in May. It's the oldest park in town

Directions: 101 exit Garden, inland to Sola

Contact: 897-1928 or www.sbparksandrecreation.com

Ventura County Fair

Why go? It's a shorter drive than to Santa Maria, and includes Destruction Derby (the epitome of intelligent entertainment), pig races, exhibits, midway, tons of farmyard animals, rodeo . . . classic fair stuff! Seems like it's always held for 10 days ending on Fiesta weekend.

Directions: 101 South 30 minutes, exit Ventura Avenue, turn left, then park free where ever you can and follow pedestrians under the freeway to the fairgrounds' north/west entrance. That way you don't get stuck in the kiddie rides first thing! Save them for last! More fun is to take Amtrak south and it stops at the fairgrounds, but don't miss the last train home!

Contact: 648-3376 or www.venturacountyfair.org

Old Spanish Days Fiesta/Santa Barbara Fiesta

Why go? Confetti eggs to break over your friend's head in De La Guerra Plaza are a must, if you don't mind crowds. Outdoor market, music concerts, dancing every day and evening in De La Guerra Plaza: Folk Dancing (Saturday evening) in the Courthouse Sunken Garden

Feel vertigo in the funhouse at August's Ventura County Fair.

(Santa Barbara Street at Anapamu Street) is the premier event during Fiesta. The Children's Parade down State Street features Santa Barbara's children dressed in costume and celebrating Santa Barbara's Old Spanish Days. The first weekend in August, Thursday through Sunday. (The three biggest events are Friday's Fiesta parade down State Street, Saturday's Children's Parade down State Street, and folk dancing Saturday night.)

Directions: For De La Guerra Plaza, take 101 exit Garden Street, go inland to De La Guerra and turn left. State Street parades are just inland of Highway 101. For Courthouse, Garden Street exit, turn inland to Figueroa Street, then go left one block.

Contact: 962-8101/897-1982 or www.oldspanishdays-fiesta.org

Multi-Cultural Dance & Music Festival

Why go? What child doesn't like music? Two days, 11-7, highlight dance, music and food from around the world.

Directions: Call for directions and dates.

Contact: 966-6950 or www.sbdancealliance.org

El Capitan Canyon's Summer Concerts & Barbecue

Why go? 6-9 p.m. Saturdays, Barbecue dinner, outdoor setting, fun music, it's untouchable for the family! Ya gotta go! Bring sand/beach chairs, sweatshirts.

Directions: 101 North 26 miles, exit El Capitan State Beach, follow signs to El Capitan Canyon on the right

Contact: (866) 352-2729 or www.elcapitancanyon.com

Kayakers re-enter sunlight after navigating a Santa Cruz Island arch.

September

El Capitan Canyon's Summer Concerts & Barbecue

Why go? 6-9 p.m. Saturdays, Barbecue dinner, outdoor setting, fun music, it's untouchable for the family! Ya gotta go! Bring sand/beach chairs, sweatshirts.

Directions: 101 North 26 miles, exit El Capitan State Beach, follow signs to El Capitan Canyon on the right

Contact: (866) 352-2729 or www.elcapitancanyon.com

Depot Day at South Coast Railroad Museum

Why go? It's the annual celebration and commemoration of preserving the old railroad depot in Goleta which was moved to this site. Entertainment, handcar rides, a barbecue and more.

Directions: 101 North, exit Los Carneros Rd., turn toward the mountains, take your second right to 300 North Los Carneros Rd.

Contact: 964-3540 or www.goletadepot.org

Zoo-B-Que

Why go? Camel rides! Food, puppet shows, magicians, a great family event! 4:30-7:30 p.m. and it's one of the Zoo's major fundraisers.

Directions: 101 exit Milpas towards ocean, left onto Cabrillo, left at the next signal onto Ninos Drive, right into Zoo.

Contact: 962-5339 or www.santabarbarazoo.org

Sandcastle & Sculpting Festival

Why go? From 11-6 Santa Barbara's biggest annual sand castle and sculpting contest and festival will show your child how it's done!

Directions: 101 South exit Milpas towards ocean, left onto Cabrillo and it's on your right at East Beach

Contact: 966-3979 or www.sandcastlefestival.com

Renaissance Faire with a Pirate Flair

Why go? Your munchkin has a jones for Pirates. You like seeing grown adults dressed and acting like pirates. It's cool. Every child contestant wins a prize in the costume contest.

Directions: 101 South, exit Highway 150, it's 30 miles. Saturday and Sunday, 10-6.

Contact: 496-6036 or www.goldcoastfestivals.com

Santa Barbara Smooth Jazz Festival

Why go? The setting at the Zoo and fundraising for the zoo.

Directions: See contact information.

Contact: 962-55339 or www.smoothjazzfestival.com

Plan beach rides in October and November on extreme minus tides!

October

Chumash Inter-Tribal Pow Wow

Why go? Top American Indian dancers and drum groups for two days from 10-6, including, arts, crafts, food, jungle gym play area for children, fishing. This is the most amount of culture you can get without leaving the country. Teach your child respect for Native Americans and another culture. Free.

Directions: 101 North 4 miles, exit 154 North 13 miles to Live Oak Campground, 4600 Highway 154.

Contact: 688-7997 or www.santaynezchumash.org or www.powwows.com

La Purísima Mission State Historic Park Candlelight Tours

Why go at night in Autumn to the most completely restored Mission in California, near Lompoc? It could be the most educational thing in this book. Docents in period dress guide you by candlelight to about 10 different settings where historical re-enactments from the missionary days are carried out by volunteers. Fantastic! Includes dinner, and it must be reserved by mail order only before July 1. Most ideal for Fourth Graders studying California history. The evening birthday event in December features hundreds of candles lighting the walkways between buildings. With a lot of open space around it, with no other buildings, it's truer to form than other Missions. There are daylight events and self-guided tours all year long.

Contact: 733-3713 or www.lapurisimamission.org

Danish Days

Why go? Aebleskivers, plain and simple. It's a tasty Danish treat, but there's also a parade, folk dancing, music, storytelling, craft demonstrations, and the windmills and atmosphere make you feel like you're in Denmark.

Directions: 101 North, exit Highway 154 north 24 miles, left onto 246 to Solvang.

Contact: 688-6144 or www.solvangcc.com or www.solvangusa.com

Avocado Festival

Why go? You love avocados, you need a festival, you like Carpinteria

Directions: 101 South, exit Linden Avenue, turn right and you're in the middle of it!

Contact: 684-0038 or www.avofest.com

Flamenco Arts Festival

Why go? Much of Santa Barbara's heritage comes from Spain, the birthplace of flamenco. Arts education programs introduce children and adults to the art of flamenco, through some of its biggest names, actually here in Santa Barbara! It's a look into their training, achievements and what flamenco has meant to their lives.

Directions: 101, exit Garden inland to Canon Perdido, left to 33 E. Canon Perdido St.

Contact: 963-0761/ www.lobero.com or www.flamencoarts.org /967-4164

Santa Barbara Harbor and Seafood Festival

Why go? The setting, the food, the people watching from 10-5, Saturday only, started about 2001

Directions: 101, exit Castillo/Bath, turn toward ocean, right on Cabrillo Boulevard, next left into harbor.

Contact: 897-1962 or www.santabarbaraca.gov/government/departments/waterfront

El Capitan Canyon's Summer Concerts & Barbecue

Why go? 6-9 p.m. Saturdays, Barbecue dinner, outdoor setting, fun music, it's untouchable for the family! Ya gotta go! Bring sand/beach chairs, sweatshirts.

Directions: 101 North 26 miles, exit El Capitan State Beach, follow signs to El Capitan Canyon on the right

Contact: (866) 352-2729 or www.elcapitancanyon.com

Lemon Festival

Why go? It starts with lemon meringue pie and lemonade, and there are games, music and every conceivable thing lemon-related. Saturday 10-9 and Sunday 10-5

Directions: 101 North 10 minutes, exit Storke Road towards ocean, right at Girsh Park, Goleta. (Also 101 North 10 minutes exit Los Carneros, right to train depot, magicians, jugglers, clowns, petting zoo, food, crafts, music, ride the antique fire engine.)

Contact: 967-4618 or www.lemonfestival.com or www.goletavalley.com

Santa Barbara Ocean Film Festival

Why go? You can teach your child to be an ambassador for the environment and teach them respect for the ocean while sitting in a theater. It's a competitive film-making event all weekend. It includes everything ocean. Review which films would be most age-appropriate.

Films have featured skim boarding, whales, dolphins, dugongs, diving, sailing, fishing, swimming and sailboarding.

Contact: 962-8404 or www.sboceanfilmfestival.com

Cat Show

Why go? You'll understand when you get there! Two days!

Directions: 101 North 3 miles, exit Las Positas turn right into the parking lot.

Contact: 687-0766 or www.earlwarren.com

Boo at the Zoo

Why go? Fantastic children-to-12 activities for the three days surrounding Halloween. Plus there is an extra-scary area for the bravest of children and adults! Well worth the effort.

Directions: 101 South one mile, exit Milpas St., right at the light, after you cross the railroad tracks turn left 1/3 mile to the zoo on your left.

Contact 962-6310 / 962-5339 or www.santabarbarazoo.org

November

Solvang Winterfest Celebration

Why go? Solvang is the "Danish Capital of America," and this is a Yule-tide celebration from mid-November until Christmas, featuring Santa, thousands of twinkling lights, events and pageantry. Take the Honen Street Car Tour aboard an authentic Danish street car pulled by Belgian horses.

Directions: 101 North to Highway 154 North, over San Marcos Pass and turn left on Highway 246 to Solvang.

Contact: 688-6144 or www.solvangusa.com

Santa Barbara Native Arts & Music Festival

Why go? Native Americans celebrate Native American Heritage Month with dancers, artisans and food at various county venues.

Contact: 403-6744

Hear your instructor/tour guide reveal Santa Cruz Island's raw beauty.

December

Tree of Light

Why go? The annual first lighting of this tree for the season is one of the most historic traditions of Santa Barbara. This Norfolk Island Pine, or Star Pine Tree, at 1019 Chapala Street is a City Landmark. If you've been to Lanai City on the island of Lanai in Hawaii, this tree may bring back fond memories of many of these magnificent trees. The two-year-old sapling was purchased by Dr. Robert F. Winchester, who Winchester Canyon was named after. He bought the sapling from noted Goleta nurseryman Joseph Sexton, previous owner of today's Sexton House adjacent to Goleta Railroad Museum. The tree was planted to celebrate the birth of Winchester's daughter. Winchester was living in Colonel William Welles Hollister's adobe residence at the site. Both Hollister Avenue and Hollister Ranch were named after that family. Starting in the 1920s, Santa Barbara community Christmas tree celebrations at this tree were headed by conservationist Pearl Chase. Chase Palm Park was later named after her contributions to Santa Barbara. The lit tree has been seen from as far as La Cumbre Peak, to ships 30 miles out to sea. As the plaque says, it's "Santa Barbara's gracious way of saying "Merry Christmas" to the world.

Directions: 101 North 1 mile, exit Carrillo Street, right at the signal to Chapala Street.

Contact for date and time: Ralph's Supermarket, 564-7000.

Downtown Holiday Parade

Why go? Bands, dancers, Santa, tree lightings on State Street; Sola to Cota 6:30 p.m. Nighttime parades are special.

Directions: 101 exit Garden, turn inland to Carrillo Street and park.

Contact: 962-2098 ext. 22 or www.santabarbaradowntown.com

Harbor Parade of Lights/Santa's Village

Why go? Usually on Sunday night, about the second weekend in December, it's about 30 boats lit up underway at night, reflected on the water; it's magical. Santa's Village (below Brophy's) 3-5 p.m., then the boat parade is from 5:30-7:15 p.m., Fireworks follow the parade.

Directions: 101 North exit Castillo, left at the signal, left at the Bath-Castillo signal towards ocean, right on Cabrillo, left into Harbor parking lot for Santa's village. View the parade of lights from the harbor or Stearns Wharf.

Contact: www.santabarbaraca.gov/resident/things/waterfront or 564-5520, 564-5531

Carpinteria Tree Lighting Ceremony

Why go? To get out without shopping, mid-December.

Directions: 101 South 11 miles, exit Linden, turn right to 700-block

Contact: 684-5405

Milpas Street Holiday Parade

Why go? This has been going on for more than 50 years! It is for children; you can't beat a parade. Starts at 10 a.m., from De La Guerra Street to Mason Street.

Directions: 101 South, exit Milpas Street, turn inland

Contact: 962-2382 or www.boysgirls.org

Trolley of Lights Tours

Why go? It's a 90-minute tour of neighborhood holiday lights starting at 6:30 p.m. in December.

Directions: Call for directions

Contact: 965-0353 or sbtrolley.com

Depending on the Timing of Your Big Event

PEP Postpartum Education for Parents

Why go? For future fun planning! Share challenges, stories and fun activity ideas with parents of children the same age as yours. There are also trained parent volunteers who teach expectant parents and offer support. You can start when you are a soon-to-be parent, or any time after that, and make lifelong friendships.

Contact: 564-3888 or www.sbpep.org

Event Notes

Setting new goals, with a professional guide and the right attitude.

Odds & Ends . . . Leftovers

Honorable mention activities include:

Santa Barbara Carriage & Western Arts Museum, only problem is, you can't climb aboard these old vehicles and saddles, 962-2353, open 9 a.m.-3 p.m. weekdays, 1-4 on Sundays and closed Saturdays.

www.sbparent.com or 448-2426, is a valuable online guide that provides Santa Barbara family resources from pregnancy through the teen years. Besides the up-to-date event calendar, it includes local perks, local businesses, kids classifieds and great information for tourists as well as South Coasters.

Santa Barbara Polo Club in Carpinteria welcomes visitors, call first for prices, (bring a picnic lunch!) for Sunday matches mid-April through mid-October, 684-6683 or www.sbpolo.com.

Fun Activities and Hotels at discounted rates are available if you arrive in Santa Barbara without a car or spend some car-free time around town, check out www.santabarbaracarfree.org.

Fast Reservations by Phone for hotels, tours, services and transportation are available through Santa Barbara Hot Spots at (800) 793-7666, Monday through Friday 9-5, Saturday 9-4 and closed Sunday. It specializes in Santa Barbara so if you have a cell phone, you no longer need to arrive without reservations! Also available on the Web at www.hotspotsusa.com.

Cachuma Lake Recreation Area offers boat rentals, camping, fishing, wildlife cruises and a nature center children's section. The two-hour cruise aboard Osprey with a naturalist is an educational, fun boat ride even if you don't see a bald eagle during winter, or other animals such as deer or wood ducks. 686-5050 or 686-5054 or www.cachuma.com.

Best Picnic Spot Award may very well go to unsung Santa Barbara City College West Campus where four tables, numerous benches, acres of grass, and Santa Barbara's tallest fountain overlook the harbor and Leadbetter Beach. Note the bridge that spans between the east and west part of the campus. The key is to go on non-school days (965-0581 to check school days) when there are fewer people around, and parking is easier. 101 North, exit Bath St., left at Haley, left again under the freeway, and turn right at W. Montecito St/Cliff Drive. Go through two signals and 200 yards after the second one, turn left into the West Campus (well marked).

Frisbee Disc Golf is available at the Evergreen Course, 101 North 11 miles, exit Storke/Glen Annie, straight through the signal onto Calle Real, right on Brandon Drive.

Pedicabs downtown are environmentally friendly and a heck of a lot of fun. Contact 320-0374 or www.sbpedicab.com

Summer Camps are extremely well listed at www.independent.com and www.newspress.com or check the Santa Barbara News-Press' and The Independent's special sections that come out in April.

Tennis is available at Las Positas Tennis Courts, 1002 Las Positas Road, Pershing Park at 100 Castillo St., Municipal Tennis Courts at 1414 Park Place off Old Coast Highway, Santa Barbara High School at 1031 Nopal St., or Oak Park at 300 W. Alamar St. Anyone 18 and older must purchase a daily or annual permit from the roaming monitor at the courts. Youth under 18 play for free. 564-5517 or www.santabarbaraca.gov/resident/recreation_and_sports/tennis.

Family Vacation Center is a week vacation for your family, staying in a family suite, doing many different activities at and around UCSB. It's like a cruise on land; it's the nearest faraway place! 893-3123 or www.familyvacationcenter.com

Batty's Batting Cages offers eight batting cages with slow to fast pitches depending on ability, 962-6666 or 226 S. Milpas St.

1,000 Steps was built in 1923 at the end of Santa Cruz Boulevard and the beach, and the lower the tide the better! Head west past Leadbetter Beach and turn left on Santa Cruz to the end. There aren't really 1,000 steps; it just feels like it!

Santa Barbara Adventure Company offers instruction or tours in rock climbing, kayaking, surfing, mountain biking, horseback riding, hiking, paragliding, and cruises at 898-0671 or www.sbadventureco.com

ATV Rentals (four-wheeled All-Terrain Vehicles) on Pismo Beach and Oceano Dunes are exciting at Steve's ATV Rentals, 75

minutes north. Use your discretion whether you drive tandem or your child drives alone. Motorized vehicles are not recommended for anyone under 16 years of age. It's open every day of the year! 474-6431 or www.stevesatv.com

Mesa Lane Beach is the most isolated beach in Santa Barbara, being the sole access to the ocean for one mile north or south. 101 North three miles, exit Las Positas Road, left onto Las Positas about 1.5 miles, left at the signal at Cliff Drive, right on Mesa Lane to the end. Lots of stairs down and dogs are accepted!

Santa Maria Valley (Children's) Discovery Museum is excellent if you're 75 minutes north on 101 and looking for fun, check out the Mayan pyramid, new shark tank, full-size tractor and toddler playground. Closed Mondays. 928-8414 or www.smvdiscoverymuseum.org

Go Launch a Rocket now! Your child will love joining you building and decorating it, and watching you launch it. Go to Hobby Central downtown, 965-2972, or California Hobbies in Goleta, 964-6563, and get a kit to build and launch your own rocket.

Mission Santa Ines in Santa Ynez Valley is educational and was the 19th Mission, built in 1804 to be a one day trip from the missions in Lompoc to the north and Santa Barbara to the south. There are picnic tables and a restroom behind the Mission. 1760 Mission Drive (Highway 246). 688-4815, www.missionsantaines.org

Laser Tag: If you have no issues with toy guns, this is a "hit." Children as young as five years old run, hide and shoot laser-beam guns indoors, and if it hits the vest of another child it registers as a score in this team-oriented game. Contact Golf N' Stuff in Ventura at 644-7131 www.golfnstuff.com, Lazer Star in Camarillo at 388-0074 www.lazerstar.org, or Ultrazone 75 miles south in Sherman Oaks, (818) 789-6620 www.zonehead.com.

Six Flags Magic Mountain/Hurricane Harbor Water Park provides world-class roller coasters and the best water park within 75 miles.

Contact: (818) 367-5965 or www.sixflags.com

Geocaching can be a bridge for video-game addicts to outdoor adventure, or it can add a high-tech game to your outings! Pronounced "geo-cashing," like a check, it's from the words geography and cache, the computer world's temporary storage area, or a camping/hiking provisions hiding place. For unlimited play around the world, your group simply enters the co-ordinates into one hand-held GPS unit

($100.00), an electronic device that can tell you the reward's latitude and longitude, within 7-21 feet. Then off you go to computer-age treasure hunting, also called Global Positioning Stash and GPS Stash Hunting. Sounds easy, right? RIGHT? www.geocaching.com.

Space Endeavour Camp is hosted by Space Endeavour Center at Vandenberg Air Force Base near Lompoc and its goal is to educate youth in space, science, mathematics and technology. Contact: 734-1747 or www.endeavours.org.

Cabins for 20? If you're looking for a rural setting over the hill for your large overnight group, Camp Whittier has nine cabins with three meals included, minimum of 20 campers. Contact: 962-6776 or www.campwhittier.org.

Only have an hour? Drive out on Stearns Wharf to the end; there are seven public picnic tables and five wooden benches waiting for you - whether it's for a snack, meal or just the view. Local shops validate your parking ticket with a purchase.

Skydive Santa Barbara is the only place within 100 miles to jump out of a plane, alone or tandem. The highest tandem jump, at 18,000 feet, is here! Contact: (877)652-5867 or www.skydivesantabarbara.com

Motorcycle and four-wheeler rentals are at Moto Loco of Santa Barbara. Contact: 899-2453 or www.motolocosb.com.

Casa del Herrero perfectly exemplifies Colonial Revival architecture and is on the list of National Register of Historic Places. Designed by George Washington Smith, it houses Spanish antiques from the 13th century, and is surrounded by 11 acres of gardens designed by Ralph Stevens, Lockwood de Forest and Peter Riedel. Tool lovers are fascinated by the previous owner's tool shop. For 10-year-olds and up. Contact: 565-5653 or casatour@silcom.com

Free Internet Access is available at the Visitors Center (make it quick) at 965-3021 or 1 Garden Street, and Santa Barbara Public Library, where there are two PCs available for 10 minutes, and 12 PCs available for 30 minutes, respectively. If you have a laptop, you can access the free wireless network. Contact: 962-7653 or www.sbplibrary.org.

Give Back for all the good you've received, and learn to value others and the environment. On your own, clean up beach/park litter, or visit retirement homes; bring retirees a snack or a sugar-free snack and ask the nurse who gets what. With a local non-profit community service organization, the options are endless! Find ideas at www.sbparent.com and search for Families Giving Back.

Wilderness Youth Project is perhaps the most valuable program in this book. The non-profit organization uses creative wilderness experiences to inspire and guide children and adults toward greater self-reliance and empathy to build a better community. Learn, donate, volunteer or register at 964-8096/www.wyp.org.

Return to Freedom, near Lompoc and also known as the American Wild Horse Sanctuary, offers opportunities to get involved, from looking at the "Just 4 Kids" page of its Web site, to donating supplies, sponsoring a horse, or experiencing its wild herd. 737-9246 or www.returntofreedom.org.

Santa Barbara Children's Museum has joyously secured an address at 125 State Street and expects to open in 2011. For information, volunteer opportunities or donations, contact: sbchildrensmuseum@gmail.com or www.sbchildrensmuseum.com.

Lil Orphan Hammies has 100 pigs for you to pet! They were homeless and abandoned. This pot-bellied pig sanctuary offers tours for school-age kids as well as volunteer opportunities. 693-9953 or www.lilorphanhammies.com

Locals looking for a quiet, flat, paved trail with an in-your-face mountain view, perfect for a one-mile wheelchair, stroller or toddler outing, should check out the city park at Sheffield Reservoir. It's not terribly developed, it features native plants and it's not signed. Dirt paths for the more ambulatory, also grace our newest park. Built in 1917 to hold 40 million gallons, an earthquake destroyed it in 1925, leading to flooding of parts of the city. Rebuilt in 1936 with a stunning Filtration Plant now listed as a Historic Landmark by the City, the reservoir was replaced by two buried 6.5-million gallon reservoirs in 2006, with the above-ground transformed into a passive park. There is a parking lot of six spaces plus a handicapped space, as well as on-street parking. Hey, you can even walk across Stanwood Drive to Fire Station 17 to ask for a tour! From Garden exit, turn inland to Haley Street, turn right and go six blocks to Milpas Street, turn right and at the second signal, turn left onto Montecito Street. At the Five Points roundabout, take Sycamore Canyon Road. Then take your first left, onto Stanwood Drive. Then take your third right, onto Mission Ridge Road, and the parking lot will be on your right.

Useful Contacts

Convention & Visitors Bureau of Santa Barbara mails out packets of information and has a user-friendly Web site. To get a 100-page visitor's guide, call (800) 927-4688. To speak with someone, call (800) 676-1266. www.santabarbaraca.com.

Santa Barbara Visitors Center has street maps, books, brochures, gifts and advice at the corner of Cabrillo Boulevard and Garden Street. Open Monday through Saturday in winter 9 a.m.-4 p.m. and Sunday 10 a.m.-4 p.m. In summer, it closes at 5 p.m. every day. If you would like a visitor's guide, call (800) 927-4688. Otherwise, call 965-3021. To see a very clear list of events this week or this year, check out its Web site at www.sbchamber.org.

Nature Activities calendar and information are at www.sbparks.org/docs/cachumacalendar.html

Santa Barbara Outdoors information, such as hiking, biking, beaches, news and activities, from Ventura to Lompoc and as far inland as Cuyama, is at www.independent.com/outdoors.

Hiking information by the man, the legend, Ray Ford, Jr., is at www.independent.com/outdoors or you can visit www.santabarbarahikes.com or www.thetrailmaster.com.

Santa Barbara Car-Free offers online maps and coupons at www.santabarbaracarfree.org.

Santa Barbara Downtown Organization for festivities, 962-2098 or www.santabarbaradowntown.com.

Santa Barbara Bicycle Coalition is invaluable for bike festivals, events and rides, www.sbbike.org.

Santa Barbara County bike map is available for free by contacting 963-7283 or www.trafficsolutions.info.

Airlines

America West and **US Airways** (800) 428-4322 or www.usairways.com
American Eagle/American Airlines (800) 433-7300 or www.aa.com
Delta Airlines (800) 221-1212 or www.delta.com
Horizon Air (800) 547-9308 or www.kayak.com

Santa Barbara Executive Jet 692-9921 or www.sbej.com
United Airlines (800) 241-6522 or www.united.com

Shuttle Services

Santa Barbara Airbus 964-7759 (800) 423-1618 or www.sbairbus.com
SuperRide Shuttle & Tours 683-9636 or (800) 977-1123 www.superride.net
Amtrak Santa Barbara Station (800) 872-7245/www.amtrak.com

Automobile Rentals

Avis Rent A Car 964-4848, (800) 831-2847/www.avis.com
Enterprise Car Rental 966-3097, (800) 736-8222/www.enterprise.com
Hertz Rent-A-Car 967-0411, (800) 654-3131/www.hertz.com
National Car Rental 967-1202, (888) 868-6207/www.nationalcar.com
Thrifty Car Rental 681-1222/www.thrifty.com

Accommodation

www.santabarbaraca.com is the Visitors Center Web site
www.hotels.com is the Web site with the most hits
www.hotspotsusa.com; local company, 564-1637, (800) 793-7666 (open Monday-Saturday)
www.coastalescapes.com, (800) 292-2222
www.santabarbara.com
www.seesantabarbara.com
www.travelocity.com
www.orbitz.com
www.expedia.com
www.cheaptickets.com

Vacation Rentals

Cabrillo Inn at the Beach, 966-1641, www.cabrillo-inn.com
Carpinteria Shores, 684-3570, www.carpinteriashores.com
Cheshire Cat Inn, 569-1610, www.cheshirecat.com
Coastal Properties, 969-1258, www.coastalrealty.com
Hotel Mar Monte, 963-0744, www.hotelmarmonte.com
Solimar Sands, 684-5613, www.solimarsands.com
Sunset Shores, 684-3682, www.carpinteriasunsetshores.com
Villa Elegante, 565-4459, www.villaelegante.com

Index

Index

Index

We'd love to hear from you!

Santa Barbara Fun For Ages 1 to 100 is the result of the input of many Santa Barbarans. We have all taken steps to ensure that this information is as accurate as possible. If you have any suggested corrections, improvements or details of your own favorite activity that you believe should be in the next edition of this book, please contact us. If we use your idea as a full-page entry, we'll send you a copy of the next edition free!

Please send all correspondence to info@santabarbarafun.net or Santa Barbara Fun, P.O. Box 50645, Santa Barbara, California 93150.

Santa Barbara Fun For Ages 1 to 100, along with contributions by Santa Barbarans, was written, photographed, compiled and edited in Santa Barbara. Now, that's local!

On a cargo truck in Zaire, after rescuing chimpanzee Dave from poachers.

About the Author

After graduating from high school, Dana Fisher set off on a road trip with a friend to have fun in Mexico and didn't turn around until he reached the state of Nayarit, south of Mazatlán. As a college student, he drove across America for the thrill of it and visited national parks along the way and in Canada. In the years following, he spent 46 months visiting 44 countries from Tasmania to Tanzania, Spain to Samoa. The entire way, his travel guidebook was his second Bible, and he learned what travelers want and need to know to make the most of their precious time.

Dana has worked as a staff photographer for newspapers including *San Diego Union-Tribune*, and has contributed to *The Christian Science Monitor, Surfer Magazine*, *Windsurf Magazine* and Japanese and French magazines.

His photographs, *Through the Eyes of Hope; The Youth of Africa*, have been exhibited at the Museum of African American History and Art in New York City, at the Moonstone Gallery in Las Vegas, and at exhibits in Simi Valley, Ventura, Santa Monica and Moorpark, California.

He married Corby, the woman of his dreams, and after honeymooning in Morocco, they settled down in Santa Barbara, California, Dana's hometown, to raise a family. They discovered Lou Grant Parent-Child Workshop, and requested the help of 140 parents – along with those in its sister program, Starr King Parent-Child Workshop in providing input for the creation of this book. Enjoy this collection of "the nearest faraway places" in and around the playground we know as Santa Barbara!

Santa Barbara Fun

ORDER FORM

Book price including tax and shipping: $25.00 per book

Number of books you are ordering: ______ × $25.00

Total Payment: __________________

Payment options: Visa/MasterCard or Money Order

Money Orders payable to: Santa Barbara Fun

Circle credit card option: Visa / MasterCard

Name on Credit Card ____

Credit Card # ____

Expiration Date ____________________ Security Code ________

Billing Address: ____

____

City ________________________________ State_____ Zip ______________

Phone ____

Shipping Address (if different from billing address)

____

City ________________________________ State_____ Zip ______________

Mail your order form and payment to:

Santa Barbara Fun
Post Office Box 50645
Santa Barbara, California 93150

or

Fax your order form to:

805-969-4128

You may also order Santa Barbara Fun For Ages 1 to 100 at our Web site,
www.santabarbarafun.net